RITE OF MARRIAGE

THE ROMAN RITUAL

revised by decree of the Second Vatican Ecumenical Council
and published by authority of Pope Paul VI

THE
RITE OF MARRIAGE

**ENGLISH TRANSLATION APPROVED BY
THE NATIONAL CONFERENCE OF CATHOLIC BISHOPS
AND CONFIRMED BY THE APOSTOLIC SEE**

English Translation Prepared by the
International Commission on English in the Liturgy

CATHOLIC BOOK PUBLISHING CORP.
NEW JERSEY

NIHIL OBSTAT:

Daniel V. Flynn, J.C.D.

Censor Librorum

IMPRIMATUR:

Joseph P. O'Brien, S.T.D

Vicar General, Archdiocese of New York

August 28, 1970

Published by authority of the Bishops' Conference on the Liturgy, National Conference of Catholic Bishops

(T-238)

ISBN 978-0-89942-238-1

Printed in Korea

www.catholicbookpublishing.com

CONTENTS

SACRED CONGREGATION OF RITES

Prot. n. R 23/969

DECREE

The rite for celebrating marriage has been revised according to the decrees of the Constitution on the Sacred Liturgy, in order that this richer rite would more clearly signify the grace of the sacrament and that the responsibilities of the married couple would be better taught. This revision has been carried out by the Consilium for the Implementation of the Constitution on the Sacred Liturgy.

By his apostolic authority, Pope Paul VI has approved this rite and directs that it be published. Therefore this sacred Congregation, acting on the special mandate of the Holy Father, publishes this rite and directs that it be used from July 1, 1969.

Anything to the contrary notwithstanding.

From the Congregation of Rites, March 19, 1969, solemnity of Saint Joseph, husband of the Blessed Virgin Mary.

Benno Card. Gut
Prefect of S.R.C.
President of the Consilium

✠ Ferdinando Antonelli
Titular Archbishop of Idicra
Secretary of S.R.C.

INTRODUCTION

IMPORTANCE AND DIGNITY OF THE SACRAMENT OF MATRIMONY

1. Married Christians, in virtue of the sacrament of matrimony, signify and share in the mystery of that unity and fruitful love which exists between Christ and his Church;[1] they help each other to attain to holiness in their married life and in the rearing and education of their children; and they have their own special gift among the people of God.[2]

2. Marriage arises in the covenant of marriage, or irrevocable consent, which each partner freely bestows on and accepts from the other. This intimate union and the good of the children impose total fidelity on each of them and argue for an unbreakable oneness between them. Christ the Lord raised this union to the dignity of a sacrament so that it might more clearly recall and more easily reflect his own unbreakable union with his Church.[3]

3. Christian couples, therefore, nourish and develop their marriage by undivided affection, which wells up from the fountain of divine love, while, in a merging of human and divine love, they remain faithful in body and in mind, in good times as in bad.[4]

4. By their very nature, the institution of matrimony and wedded love are ordained for the procreation and education of children and find in them their ultimate crown. Therefore, married Christians, while not considering the other purposes of marriage of less account, should be steadfast and ready to cooperate with the love of the Creator and Savior, who through them will constantly enrich and enlarge his own family.[5]

5. A priest should bear in mind these principles of faith, both in his instructions to those about to be married and when giving the homily during the marriage ceremony. He should relate his instructions to the texts of the sacred readings.[6]

The bridal couple should be given a review of the fundamentals of Christian doctrine. This may include instruction on the teachings about marriage and the family, on the rites used in the celebration of the sacrament itself, and on the prayers and readings. In this way the bridegroom and the bride will receive far greater benefit from the celebration.

6. In the celebration of marriage (which normally should be within the Mass), certain elements should be stressed, especially the liturgy of the word, which shows the importance of Christian marriage in the history of salvation and the duties and responsibility of the couple in caring for the holiness of their children. Also of supreme importance are the consent of the contracting parties, which the priest asks and receives; the special nuptial blessing for the bride and for the marriage covenant; and finally, the reception of holy communion by the groom and the bride, and by all present, by which their love is nourished and all are lifted up into communion with our Lord and with one another.[7]

7. Priests should first of all strengthen and nourish the faith of those about to be married, for the sacrament of matrimony presupposes and demands faith.[8]

CHOICE OF RITE

8. In a marriage between a Catholic and a baptized person who is not Catholic, the regulations which appear below in the rite of marriage outside Mass (nos. 39-54) shall be observed. If suitable, and if the Ordinary of the place gives permission, the rite for celebrating marriage within Mass (nos. 19-38) may be used, except that, according to the general law, communion is not given to the non-Catholic.

In a marriage between a Catholic and one who is not baptized, the rite which appears in nos. 55-56 is to be followed.

9. Furthermore, priests should show special consideration to those who take part in liturgical celebrations or hear the gospel only on the occasion of a wedding, either because they are not Catholics, or because they are Catholics who rarely, if ever, take part in the eucharist or seem to have abandoned the practice of their faith. Priests are ministers of Christ's gospel to everyone.

10. In the celebration of matrimony, apart from the liturgical laws providing for due honors to civil authorities, no special honors are to be paid to any private persons or classes of person, whether in the ceremonies or by external display.[9]

11. Whenever marriage is celebrated during Mass, white vestments are worn and the wedding Mass is used. If the marriage is celebrated on a Sunday or solemnity, the Mass of the day is used with the nuptial blessing and, where appropriate, the special final blessing.

The liturgy of the word is extremely helpful in emphasizing the meaning of the sacrament and the obligations of marriage. When the wedding Mass may not be used, one of the readings in nos. 67-105 should be chosen, except from Holy Thursday to Easter and on the feasts of Christmas, Epiphany, Ascension, Pentecost, Corpus Christi, and other holydays of obligation. On the Sundays of the Christmas season and throughout the year, in Masses which are not parish Masses, the wedding Mass may be used without change.

When a marriage is celebrated during Advent or Lent or other days of penance, the parish priest should advise the couple to take into consideration the special nature of these times.

PREPARATION OF LOCAL RITUALS

12. In addition to the faculty spoken of below in no. 17 for regions where the Roman Ritual for matrimony is used, particular rituals shall be prepared, suitable for the customs and needs of individual areas, according to the principle of art. 63b and 77 of the Constitution on the Sacred Liturgy. These are to be reviewed by the Apostolic See.

In making adaptations, the following points must be remembered:

13. The formulas of the Roman Ritual may be adapted or, as the case may be, filled out (including the questions before the consent and the actual words of consent).

When the Roman Ritual has several optional formulas, local rituals may add other formulas of the same type.

14. Within the rite of the sacrament of matrimony, the arrangement of its parts may be varied. If it seems more suitable, even the questions before the consent may be omitted as long as the priest asks and receives the consent of the contracting parties.

15. After the exchange of rings, the crowning or veiling of the bride may take place according to local custom.

In any region where the joining of hands or the blessing or exchange of rings does not fit in with the practice of the people, the conference of bishops may allow these rites to be omitted or other rites substituted.

16. As for the marriage cusoms of nations that are now receiving the gospel for the first time, whatever is good and is not indissolubly bound up with superstition and error should be sympathetically considered and, if possible, preserved intact. Sometimes the Church admits such things into the liturgy itself, as long as they harmonize with its true and authentic spirit.[10]

RIGHT TO PREPARE A COMPLETELY NEW RITE

17. Each conference of bishops may draw up its own marriage rite suited to the usages of the place and people and approved by the Apostolic See. The rite must always conform to the law that the priest assisting at such marriages must ask for and receive the consent of the contracting parties,[11] and the nuptial blessing should always be given.[12]

18. Among peoples where the marriage ceremonies customarily take place in the home, sometimes over a period of several days, these customs should be adapted to the Christian spirit and to the liturgy. In such cases the conference of bishops, according to the pastoral needs of the people, may allow the sacramental rite to be celebrated in the home.

NOTES

1. Ephesians 5:32.
2. 1 Corinthians 7:7; II Vatican Council, Dogmatic Constitution on the Church, *Lumen Gentium,* 11.
3. II Vatican Council, Constitution on the Church in the Modern World, *Gaudium et Spes,* 48.
4. *Ibid.,* 48, 49.
5. *Ibid.,* 48, 50.
6. II Vatican Council, Constitution on the Sacred Liturgy, *Sacrosanctum Concilium,* 52; S.C.R., Instruction *Inter Oecumenici,* no. 54: AAS 56 (1964) 890.
7. II Vatican Council, Decree on the Apostolate of the Laity, *Apostolicam actuositatem,* 3; Dogmatic Constitution on the Church, *Lumen Gentium,* 12.
8. II Vatican Council, Constitution on the Sacred Liturgy, *Sacrosanctum Concilium,* 59.
9. *Ibid.,* 32.
10. *Ibid.,* 37.
11. *Ibid.,* 77.
12. *Ibid.,* 78.

CHAPTER I

RITE FOR CELEBRATING MARRIAGE DURING MASS

ENTRANCE RITE

19. At the appointed time, the priest, vested for Mass, goes with the ministers to the door of the church or, if more suitable, to the altar. There he greets the bride and bridegroom in a friendly manner, showing that the Church shares their joy.

Where it is desirable that the rite of welcome be omitted, the celebration of marriage begins at once with the Mass.

20. If there is a procession to the altar, the ministers go first, followed by the priest, and then the bride and bridegroom. According to local custom, they may be escorted by at least their parents and the two witnesses. Meanwhile, the entrance song is sung.

LITURGY OF THE WORD

21. The liturgy of the word is celebrated according to the rubics. There may be three readings, the first of them from the Old Testament.

22. After the gospel, the priest gives a homily drawn from the sacred text. He speaks about the mystery of Christian marriage, the dignity of wedded love, the grace of the sacrament and the responsibilities of married people, keeping in mind the circumstances of this particular marriage.

RITE OF MARRIAGE

23. All stand, including the bride and bridegroom, and the priest addresses them in these or similar words:

My dear friends, * you have come together in this church so that the Lord may seal and strengthen your love in the presence of the Church's minister and this community. Christ abundantly

---

*At the discretion of the priest, other words which seem more suitable under the circumstances, such as friends, dearly beloved, brethren, may be used. This also applies to parallel instances in the liturgy.

blesses this love. He has already consecrated you in baptism and now he enriches and strengthens you by a special sacrament so that you may assume the duties of marriage in mutual and lasting fidelity. And so, in the presence of the Church, I ask you to state your intentions.

24. The priest then questions them about their freedom of choice, faithfulness to each other, and the acceptance and upbringing of children:

N. and N. have you come here freely and without reservation to give yourselves to each other in marriage?

Will you love and honor each other as man and wife for the rest of your lives?

The following question may be omitted if, for example, the couple is advanced in years.

Will you accept children lovingly from God, and bring them up according to the law of Christ and his Church?

Each answers the questions separately.

Consent

25. The priest invites the couple to declare their consent:

Since it is your intention to enter into marriage, join your right hands, and declare your consent before God and his Church.

They join hands.

A The bridegroom says:

I, N., take you, N., to be my wife. I promise to be true to you in good times and in bad, in sickness and in health. I will love you and honor you all the days of my life.

The bride says:

I, N., take you, N., to be my husband. I promise to be true to you in good times and in bad, in sickness and in health. I will love you and honor you all the days of my life.

B

In dioceses of the United States the following form may be used:

The bridegroom says:

I, N., take you, N., for my lawful wife, to have and to hold, from this day forward, for better, for worse, for richer, for poorer, in sickness and in health, until death do us part.

The bride says:

I, N., take you, N., for my lawful husband, to have and to hold, from this day forward, for better, for worse, for richer, for poorer, in sickness and in health, until death do us part.

A

If, however, it seems preferable for pastoral reasons, the priest may obtain consent from the couple through questions.

First he asks the bridegroom:

N., do you take N. to be your wife? Do you promise to be true to her in good times and in bad, in sickness and in health, to love her and honor her all the days of your life?

The bridegroom: **I do.**

Then he asks the bride:

N., do you take N. to be your husband? Do you promise to be true to him in good times and in bad, in sickness and in health, to love him and honor him all the days of your life?

The bride: **I do.**

B

In dioceses of the United States the following form may be used:

First he asks the bridegroom:

N., do you take N. for your lawful wife, to have and to hold, from this day forward, for better, for worse, for richer, for poorer, in sickness and in health, until death do you part?

The bridegroom: **I do.**

Then he asks the bride:

N., do you take N. for your lawful husband, to have and to hold, from this day forward, for better, for worse, for richer, for poorer, in sickness and in health, until death do you part?

The bride: **I do.**

If pastoral necessity demands it, the conference of bishops may decree, in virtue of the faculty in no. 17, that the priest should always obtain the consent of the couple through questions.

26. Receiving their consent, the priest says:

You have declared your consent before the Church. May the Lord in his goodness strengthen your consent and fill you both with his blessings.

What God has joined, men must not divide.

℟. **Amen.**

Blessing and Exchange of Rings

27. Priest:

A

May the Lord bless ✠ these rings
which you give to each other
as the sign of your love and fidelity.

℟. **Amen.**

B **(110)**

Lord, bless these rings which we bless ✠ in your name.
Grant that those who wear them
may always have a deep faith in each other.
May they do your will
and always live together
in peace, good will, and love.

We ask this through Christ our Lord.

℟. **Amen.**

C **(111)**

Lord,
bless ✠ and consecrate N. and N.
in their love for each other.
May these rings be a symbol
of true faith in each other,
and always remind them of their love.
Through Christ our Lord.
℟. **Amen.**

28. The bridegroom places his wife's ring on her ring finger.

He may say:

N., **take this ring as a sign of my love and fidelity. In the name of the Father, and of the Son, and of the Holy Spirit.**

The bride places her husband's ring on his ring finger. She may say:

N., **take this ring as a sign of my love and fidelity. In the name of the Father, and of the Son, and of the Holy Spirit.**

29. The general intercessions (prayer of the faithful) follow, using formulas approved by the conference of bishops. If the rubrics call for it, the profession of faith is said after the general intercessions.

LITURGY OF THE EUCHARIST

30. The Order of Mass is followed, with the following changes. During the offertory, the bride and bridegroom may bring the bread and wine to the altar.

31. **Proper preface** (see nos. 115-117). (See page 124)

32. When the Roman canon is used, the special **Hanc igitur** is said (no. 118).

Nuptial Blessing

33. After the Lord's Prayer, the prayer Deliver us is omitted. The priest faces the bride and bridegroom and, with hands joined, says:

A

My dear friends, let us turn to the Lord and pray
that he will bless with his grace this woman (or N.)
now married in Christ to this man (or N.)
and that (**through the sacrament of the body and blood of Christ,**)
he will unite in love the couple he has joined in this holy bond.

All pray silently for a short while. Then the priest extends his hands and continues:

Father, by your power you have made everything out of nothing.
In the beginning you created the universe
and made mankind in your own likeness.
You gave man the constant help of woman
so that man and woman should no longer be two, but one flesh,
and you teach us that what you have united
may never be divided.

Father, you have made the union of man and wife so holy a mystery that it symbolizes the marriage of Christ and his Church.

Father, by your plan man and woman are united,
and married life has been established
as the one blessing that was not forfeited by original sin
or washed away in the flood.

Look with love upon this woman, your daughter,
now joined to her husband in marriage.
She asks your blessing.
Give her the grace of love and peace.
May she always follow the example of the holy women
whose praises are sung in the scriptures.

May her husband put his trust in her
and recognize that she is his equal
and the heir with him to the life of grace.
May he always honor her and love her
as Christ loves his bride, the Church.

Father, keep them always true to your commandments.
Keep them faithful in marriage
and let them be living examples of Christian life.

Give them the strength which comes from the gospel
so that they may be witnesses of Christ to others.
(Bless them with children
and help them to be good parents.
May they live to see their children's children.)
And, after a happy old age,
grant them fullness of life with the saints
in the kingdom of heaven.

We ask this through Christ our Lord.

℟. **Amen.**

34. If one or both of the parties will not be receiving communion, the words in the introduction to the nuptial blessing, through the sacrament of the body and blood of Christ, may be omitted.

If desired, in the prayer Father, by your power, two of the first three paragraphs may be omitted, keeping only the paragraph which corresponds to the reading of the Mass.

In the last paragraph of this prayer, the words in parentheses may be omitted whenever circumstances suggest it, if, for example, the couple is advanced in years.

Other forms of the nuptial blessing:

B (120)

In the following prayer, either the paragraph Holy Father, you created mankind or the paragraph Father, to reveal the plan of your love, may be omitted, keeping only the paragraph which corresponds to the reading of the Mass.

Let us pray to the Lord for N. and N.
who come to God's altar at the beginning of their married life
so that they may always be united in love for each other
(as now they share in the body and blood of Christ).

All pray silently for a short while. Then the priest extends his hands and continues:

Holy Father, you created mankind in your own image
and made man and woman to be joined as husband and wife
in union of body and heart
and so fulfill their mission in this world.

Father, to reveal the plan of your love,
you made the union of husband and wife
an image of the covenant between you and your people.

In the fulfillment of this sacrament,
the marriage of Christian man and woman
is a sign of the marriage between Christ and the Church.
Father, stretch out your hand, and bless N. and N.

Lord, grant that as they begin to live this sacrament
they may share with each other the gifts of your love
and become one in heart and mind
as witnesses to your presence in their marriage.
Help them to create a home together
(and give them children to be formed by the gospel
and to have a place in your family).

Give your blessing to N., your daughter,

so that she may be a good wife (and mother),
caring for the home,
faithful in love for her husband,
generous and kind.
Give your blessings to N., your son,
so that he may be a faithful husband
(and a good father).

Father, grant that as they come together to your table on earth,
so they may one day have the joy of sharing your feast in heaven.

We ask this through Christ our Lord.
℟. **Amen.**

C **(121)**

My dear friends, let us ask God
for his continued blessings upon this bridegroom and his bride
(or N. and N.).

All pray silently for a short while. Then the priest extends his hands and continues:

Holy Father, creator of the universe,
maker of man and woman in your own likeness,
source of blessing for married life,
we humbly pray to you for this woman
who today is united with her husband in this sacrament of marriage.

May your fullest blessing come upon her and her husband
so that they may together rejoice in your gift of married love
(and enrich your Church with their children).

Lord, may they both praise you when they are happy
and turn to you in their sorrows.
May they be glad that you help them in their work
and know that you are with them in their need.

May they pray to you in the community of the Church,
and be your witnesses in the world.
May they reach old age in the company of their friends,
and come at last to the kingdom of heaven.

We ask this through Christ our Lord.
℟. Amen.

35. At the words Let us offer each other the sign of peace, the marriage couple and all present show their peace and love for one another in an appropriate way.

36. The married couple may receive communion under both kinds.

SOLEMN BLESSING

37. Before blessing the people at the end of Mass, the priest blesses the bride and bridegroom, using one of the forms below:

A (125)

God the eternal Father keep you in love with each other,
so that the peace of Christ may stay with you
and be always in your home.
℟. Amen.

May (your children bless you,)
your friends console you
and all men live in peace with you.
℟. Amen.

May you always bear witness to the love of God in this world
so that the afflicted and the needy
will find in you generous friends,
and welcome you into the joys of heaven.
℟. Amen.

And may almighty God bless you all,
the Father, and the Son, ✠ and the Holy Spirit.
℟. Amen.

B **(126)**

May God, the almighty Father,
give you his joy
and bless you (in your children).
℟. **Amen.**

May the only Son of God have mercy on you
and help you in good times and in bad.
℟. **Amen.**

May the Holy Spirit of God
always fill your hearts with his love.
℟. **Amen.**

And may almighty God bless you all,
the Father, and the Son, ✠ and the Holy Spirit.
℟. **Amen.**

C **(127)**

May the Lord Jesus, who was a guest at the wedding in Cana,
bless you and your families and friends.
℟. **Amen.**

May Jesus, who loved his Church to the end,
always fill your hearts with his love.
℟. **Amen.**

May he grant that, as you believe in his resurrection,
so you may wait for him in joy and hope.
℟. **Amen.**

And may almighty God bless you all,
the Father, and the Son, ✠ and the Holy Spirit.
℟. **Amen.**

D In the diocese of the United States the following form may be used:

May almighty God, with his Word of blessing, unite your hearts in the never-ending bond of pure love. ℟. **Amen.**

May your children bring you happiness, and may your generous love for them be returned to you, many times over. ℟. **Amen.**

May the peace of Christ live always in your hearts and in your home.

May you have true friends to stand by you, both in joy and in sorrow.

May you be ready and willing to help and comfort all who come to you in need.

And may the blessings promised to the compassionate be yours in abundance. ℟. **Amen.**

May you find happiness and satisfaction in your work.

May daily problems never cause you undue anxiety, nor the desire for earthly possessions dominate your lives.

But may your hearts' first desire be always the good things waiting for you in the life of heaven. ℟. **Amen.**

May the Lord bless you with many happy years together, so that you may enjoy the rewards of a good life.

And after you have served him loyally in his kingdom on earth, may he welcome you to his eternal kingdom in heaven. ℟. Amen.

And may almighty God bless you all,
the Father, and the Son, ✠ and the Holy Spirit.
℟. Amen.

38. In two or more marriages are celebrated at the same time, the questioning before the consent, the consent itself, and the acceptance of consent shall always be done individually for each couple; the rest, including the nuptial blessing, is said once of all, using the plural form.

CHAPTER II

RITE FOR CELEBRATING MARRIAGE OUTSIDE MASS[13]

INTRODUCTORY RITES AND LITURGY OF THE WORD

39. At the appointed time, the priest, wearing surplice and white stole (or white cope, if desired), proceeds with the ministers to the door of the church or, if more suitable, to the altar. There he greets the bride and bridegroom in a friendly manner, showing that the Church shares their joy.

Where it is desirable that the rite of welcome be omitted, the celebration of matrimony begins at once with the liturgy of the word.

40. If there is a procession to the altar, the ministers go first, followed by the priest, and then the bride and bridegroom. According to local custom, they may be escorted by at least their parents and the two witnesses. Meanwhile, the entrance song is sung.

Then the people are greeted, and the prayer is offered, unless, a brief pastoral exhortation seems more desirable.[14]

41. The liturgy of the word takes place in the usual manner. There may be three readings, the first of them from the Old Testament.

42. After the gospel, the priest gives a homily drawn from the sacred text. He speaks about the mystery of Christian marriage, the dignity of wedded love, the grace of the sacrament, and the responsibilities of married people, keeping in mind the circumstances of this particular marriage.

RITE OF MARRAGE

43. All stand, including the bride and bridegroom, and the priest addresses them in these or similar words:

My dear friends, you have come together in this church so that the Lord may seal and strengthen your love in the presence of the Church's minister and this community. Christ abundantly blesses this love. He has already consecrated you in baptism and now he enriches and strengthens you by a special sacrament so

that you may assume the duties of marriage in mutual and lasting fidelity. And so, in the presence of the Church, I ask you to state your intentions.

44. The priest then questions them about their freedom of choice, faithfulness to each other, and the acceptance and upbringing of children:

N. and N., have you come here freely and without reservation to give yourselves to each other in marriage?

Will you love and honor each other as man and wife for the rest of your lives?

The following question may be omitted if, for example, the couple is advanced in years.

Will you accept children lovingly from God, and bring them up according to the law of Christ and his Church?

Each answers the questions separately.

Consent

45. The priest invites them to declare their consent:

Since it is your intention to enter into marriage, join your right hands, and declare your consent before God and his Church.

They join hands.

A The bridegroom says:

I, N., take you, N., to be my wife. I promise to be true to you in good times and in bad, in sickness and in health. I will love you and honor you all the days of my life.

The bride says:

I, N., take you, N., to be my husband. I promise to be true to you in good times and in bad, in sickness and in health. I will love you and honor you all the days of my life.

B

In dioceses of the United States the following form may be used:

The bridegroom says:

I, N., take you, N., for my lawful wife, to have and to hold, from this day forward, for better, for worse, for richer, for poorer, in sickness and in health, until death do us part.

The bride says:

I, N., take you, N., for my lawful husband, to have and to hold, from this day forward, for better, for worse, for richer, for poorer, in sickness and in health, until death do us part.

If, however, it seems preferable for pastoral reasons, the priest may obtain consent from the couple through questions.

First he asks the bridegroom:

A

N., do you take N. to be your wife? Do you promise to be true to her in good times and in bad, in sickness and in health, to love her and honor her all the days of your life?

The bridegroom: **I do.**

Then he asks the bride:

N., do you take N. to be your husband? Do you promise to be true to him in good times and in bad, in sickness and in health, to love him and honor him all the days of your life?

The bride: **I do.**

In dioceses of the United States the following form may be used:

B

First he asks the bridegroom:

N., do you take N. for your lawful wife, to have and to hold, from this day forward, for better, for worse, for richer, for poorer, in sickness and in health, until death do you part?

The bridegroom: **I do.**

Then he asks the bride:

N., do you take N. for your lawful husband, to have and to hold, from this day forward, for better, for worse, for richer, for poorer, in sickness and in health, until death do you part?

The bride: **I do.**

If pastoral necessity demands it, the conference of bishops may decree, in virtue of the faculty in no. 17, that the priest should always obtain the consent of the couple through questions.

Receiving their consent, the priest says:

You have declared your consent before the Church. May the Lord in his goodness strengthen your consent and fill you both with his blessings.

What God has joined, men must not divide.

℟. **Amen.**

Blessing and Exchange of Rings

47. Priest:

May the Lord bless ✠ these rings which you give to each other as the sign of your love and fidelity.

℟. **Amen.**

For the other forms of the blessing of rings, see nos. 110, 111. (See page 122)

48. The bridegroom places his wife's ring on her ring finger. He may say:

N., take this ring as a sign of my love and fidelity. In the name of the Father, and of the Son, and of the Holy Spirit.

The bride places her husband's ring on his ring finger. She may say:

N., take this ring as a sign of my love and fidelity. In the name of the Father, and of the Son, and of the Holy Spirit.

General Intercessions and Nuptial Blessings

49. The general intercessions (prayer of the faithful) and the blessing of the couple take place in this order:

a) First the priest uses the invitatory of any blessing of the couple (see the first part of no. 33, 120, 121) or any other, taken from the approved formulas for the general intercessions.

b) Immediately after the invitatory, there can be either a brief silence, or a series of petitions from the prayer of the faithful with responses by the people. All the petitions should be in harmony with the blessing which follows, but should not duplicate it.

c) Then, omitting the prayer that concludes the prayer of the faithful, the priest extends his hands and blesses the bride and bridegroom.

50. This blessing may be Father, by your power, (no. 33) or another from nos. 120, 121.

CONCLUSION OF THE CELEBRATION

51. The entire rite can be concluded with the Lord's Prayer and the blessing, whether with the simple form, May almighty God, or with one of the forms in nos. 125-127.

52. If two or more marriages are celebrated at the same time, the questioning before the consent, the consent itself, and the acceptance of consent shall always be done individually for each couple; the rest, including the nuptial blessing, is said once for all, using the plural form.

53. The rite described above should be used by a deacon who, when a priest cannot be present, has been delegated by the bishop or pastor to assist at the celebration of marriage, and to give the Church's blessing.[15]

54. If Mass cannot be celebrated and communion is to be distributed during the rite, the Lord's Prayer is said first. After communion, a reverent silence may be observed for a while, or a psalm or song of praise be sung or recited. Then comes the prayer, Lord, we who have shared (no. 123, if only the bride and bridegroom receive), or the prayer, God, who in this wondrous sacrament or other suitable prayer.

The rite ends with a blessing, either the simple formula, May almighty God bless you, or one of the forms in nos. 125-127.

NOTES

13. According to the words of the Constitution on the Sacred Liturgy, *Sacrosanctum Concilium,* repeated in no. 6 of the introduction above, the celebration of marriage normally takes place during Mass. Nevertheless, a good reason can excuse from the celebration of Mass (Sacred Congregation of Rites, Instruction, *Inter Oecumenici,* no. 70: AAS 56 (1964) 893), and sometimes even urges that Mass should be omitted. In this case the rite for celebrating marriage outside Mass should be used.
14. II Vatican Council, Sacred Congregation of Rites, Instruction *Inter Oecumenici,* no. 74: AAS 56 (1964) 894.
15. Paul VI, motu proprio, *Sacram Diaconatus Ordinem,* June 18, 1967, no. 22, 4: AAS 59 (1967) 702.

CHAPTER III

RITE FOR CELEBRATING MARRIAGE BETWEEN A CATHOLIC AND AN UNBAPTIZED PERSON

If marriage is celebrated between a Catholic and an unbaptized person (either a catechumen or a non-Christian), the rite may be performed in the church or some other suitable place and takes the following form.

Rite of Welcome and Liturgy of the Word

55. At the appointed time, the priest wearing surplice and white stole (or a white cope if desired), proceeds with the ministers to the door of the church or to another appropriate place and greets the bride and the bridegroom.

Where it is desirable that the rite of welcome be omitted, the celebration of marriage begins at once with the liturgy of the word.

56. The liturgy of the word takes place in the usual manner. There may be three readings, the first of them from the Old Testament. If circumstances make it more desirable, there may be a single reading.

57. A homily, drawn from the sacred text, is given and should speak of the obligations of marriage and other appropriate points.

RITE OF MARRIAGE

58. All stand, including the bride and the bridegroom. The priest addresses them in these or similar words:

My dear friends, you have come together in this church so that the Lord may seal and strengthen your love in the presence of the Church's minister and this community. In this way you will be strengthened to keep mutual and lasting faith with each other and to carry out the other duties of marriage. And so, in the presence of the Church, I ask you to state your intentions.

59. The priest then questions them about their freedom of choice, faithfulness to each other, and the acceptance and upbringing of children:

N. and N., have you come here freely and without reservation to give yourselves to each other in marriage?

Will you love and honor each other as man and wife for the rest of your lives?

The following question may be omitted if, for example, the couple is advanced in years.

Will you accept children lovingly from God, and bring them up according to the law of Christ and his Church?

Each answers the questions separately.

Consent

60. The priest invites them to declare their consent:

Since it is your intention to enter into marriage, join your right hands, and declare your consent before God and his Church.

They join hands.

 The bridegroom says:

I N., take you, N., to be my wife. I promise to be true to you in good times and in bad, in sickness and in health: I will love you and honor you all the days of my life.

The bride says:

I, N., take you, N., to be my husband. I promise to be true to you in good times and in bad, in sickness and in health: I will love you and honor you all the days of my life.

In dioceses of the United States the following form may be used:

The bridegroom says:

B

I, N., take you, N., for my lawful wife, to have and to hold, from this day forward, for better, for worse, for richer, for poorer, in sickness and in health, until death do us part.

The bride says:

I, N., take you, N., for my lawful husband, to have and to hold, from this day forward, for better, for worse, for richer, for poorer, in sickness and in health, until death do us part.

If, however, it seems preferable for pastoral reasons, the priest may obtain consent from the couple through questions.

First he asks the bridegroom:

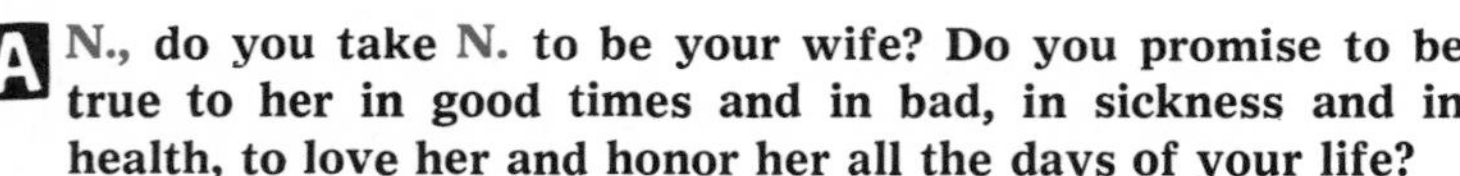

A **N., do you take N. to be your wife? Do you promise to be true to her in good times and in bad, in sickness and in health, to love her and honor her all the days of your life?**

The bridegroom: **I do.**

Then he asks the bride:

N., do you take N. to be your husband? Do you promise to be true to him in good times and in bad, in sickness and in health, to love him and honor him all the days of your life?

The bride: **I do.**

In dioceses of the United States the following form may be used:

First he asks the bridegroom:

N., do you take N. for your lawful wife, to have and to hold, from this day forward, for better, for worse, for richer, for poorer, in sickness and in health, until death do you part?

The bridegroom: **I do.**

Then he asks the bride:

N., do you take N. for your lawful husband, to have and to hold, from this day forward, for better, for worse, for richer, for poorer, in sickness and in health, until death do you part?

The bride: **I do.**

If pastoral necessity demands it, the conference of bishops may decree, in virtue of the faculty in no. 17, that the priest should always obtain the consent of the couple through questions.

61. Receiving their consent, the priest says:

You have declared your consent before the Church. May the Lord in his goodness strengthen your consent and fill you both with his blessings.

What God has joined, men must not divide.

℟. **Amen.**

Blessing and Exchange of Rings

62. If circumstances so require, the blessing and exchange of rings can be omitted. If this rite is observed, the priest says:

May the Lord bless ✠ these rings which you give to each other as the sign of your love and fidelity.

℟. **Amen.**

For other forms of the blessing of rings, see nos. 110-111.

63. The bridegroom places his wife's ring on her ring finger. He may say:

N., take this ring as a sign of my love and fidelity.
In the name of the Father, and of the Son, and of the Holy Spirit.

The bride places her husband's ring on his ring finger. She may say:

N., take this ring as a sign of my love and fidelity.
In the name of the Father, and of the Son, and of the Holy Spirit.

General Intercessions and Nuptial Blessings

64. If circumstances so require, the blessing of the bride and bridegroom can be omitted. If used, it is combined with the general intercessions (prayer of the faithful) in this order:

a) First the priest uses the invitatory of any blessing of the couple (see the first part of nos. 33, 120, 121) or any other, taken from any approved formula for the general intercess ons.

b) Immediately after the invitatory, there can be either a brief period of silence, or a series of petitions from the prayer of the faithful with responses by the people. All the petitions should be in harmony with the blessing which follows, but should not duplicate it.

c) Then, omitting the prayer that concludes the prayer of the faithful, the priest blesses the bride and bridegoom.

65. Facing them, he joins his hands and says:

My brothers and sisters, let us ask God
for his continued blessings upon this bridegroom and his bride.

All pray silently for a short while. Then the priest extends his hands and continues:

Holy Father, creator of the universe,
maker of man and woman in your own likeness,
source of blessing for the married life,
we humbly pray to you for this bride
who today is united with her husband in the bond of marriage.

May your fullest blessing come upon her and her husband
so that they may together rejoice in your gift of married love.
May they be noted for their good lives,
(and be parents filled with virtue).

Lord, may they both praise you when they are happy
and turn to you in their sorrows.
May they be glad that you help them in their work,
and know that you are with them in their need.
May they reach old age in the company of their friends,
and come at last to the kingdom of heaven.
We ask this through Christ our Lord. ℟. **Amen.**

CONCLUSION OF THE CELEBRATION

66. The rite may be concluded with the Lord's prayer (or, if the nuptial blessing has been omitted, another prayer by the priest) and a blessing using the customary form, May almighty God bless you or another formula from nos. 125-127.

CHAPTER IV

RITE FOR CELEBRATING MARRIAGE DURING MASS

INTRODUCTORY RITES

ENTRANCE RITE

At the appointed time, the priest, vested for Mass, goes with the ministers to the door of the Church or, if more suitable, to the altar. There he greets the bride and bridegroom in a friendly manner, showing that the Church shares their joy.

Where it is desirable that the rite of welcome be omitted, the celebration of marriage begins at once with the Mass.

If there is a procession to the altar, the ministers go first, followed by the priest, and then the bride and bridegroom. According to local custom, they may be escorted by at least their parents and the two witnesses. Meanwhile, the entrance song is sung.

When the priest comes to the altar, he makes the customary reverence with the ministers, kisses the altar, and (if incense is used) incenses it. Then, with the ministers, he goes to the chair.

After the entrance song, the priest and the faithful remain standing and make the sign of the cross, as the priest says:

In the name of the Father, and of the Son, and of the Holy Spirit.

The people answer:

Amen.

Then the priest, facing the people, extends his hands and greets all present with one of the following greetings:

A GREETING

The grace of our Lord Jesus Christ and the love of God and the fellowship of the Holy Spirit be with you all.

The people answer:

And also with you.

B

or the priest says:

The grace and peace of God our Father and the Lord Jesus Christ be with you.

The people answer:

Blessed be God, the Father of our Lord Jesus Christ.

or:

And also with you.

or the priest says:

The Lord be with you.

The people answer:

And also with you.

Instead of the greeting, The Lord be with you, a bishop says:

Peace be with you.

The priest, deacon, or other suitable minister may very briefly introduce the Mass of the day.

PENITENTIAL RITE

The priest invites the people to repent of their sins:

My brothers and sisters, * to prepare ourselves to celebrate the mysteries, let us call to mind our sins.

A **After a brief silence, all say:**

I confess to almighty God,
and to you, my brothers and sisters,
that I have sinned through my own fault

They strike their breast:

in my thoughts and in my words,
in what I have done,
and in what I have failed to do;
and I ask blessed Mary, ever virgin,
all the angels and saints,
and you, my brothers and sisters,
to pray for me to the Lord our God.

The priest says the absolution:

May almighty God have mercy on us,
forgive us our sins,
and bring us to everlasting life.

The people answer:

Amen.

At the discretion of the priest, other words which seem more suitable under the circumstances, such as friends, dearly beloved, brethren, may be used. This also applies to parallel instances in the liturgy.

B

The priest invites the people to repent of their sins:

My brothers and sisters, to prepare ourselves to celebrate the sacred mysteries, let us call to mind our sins.

After a brief silence, the priest says:

Lord, we have sinned against you.

The people answer:

Lord, have mercy.

Priest:

Lord, show us your mercy and love.

People:

And grant us your salvation.

The priest says the absolution:

May almighty God have mercy on us,
forgive us our sins,
and bring us to everlasting life.

The people answer:

Amen.

C

The priest invites the people to repent of their sins:

My brothers and sisters, to prepare ourselves to celebrate the sacred mysteries, let us call to mind our sins:

After a brief silence, the priest (or other suitable minister) makes the following or other invocations, with **Lord, have mercy.**

You were sent to heal the contrite:
Lord, have mercy.

The people answer:

Lord, have mercy.

Priest:

You came to call sinners:
Christ, have mercy.

People:

Christ, have mercy.

Priest:

You plead for us at the right hand of the Father:
Lord, have mercy.

People:

Lord, have mercy.

The priest says the absolution:

May almighty God have mercy on us,
forgive us our sins,
and bring us to everlasting life.

The people answer:

Amen.

The invocations, **Lord, have mercy,** follow, unless they have already been used in one of the forms of the act of penance.

℣. **Lord, have mercy.** ℟. Lord, have mercy.
℣. **Christ, have mercy.** ℟. Christ, have mercy.
℣. **Lord, have mercy.** ℟. Lord, have mercy.

Then (when it is prescribed) this hymn is said or sung:

Glory to God in the highest,
and peace to his people on earth.
Lord God, heavenly King,
almighty God and Father,
we worship you, we give you thanks,
we praise you for your glory.

Lord Jesus Christ, only Son of the Father,
Lord God, Lamb of God,
you take away the sin of the world:
have mercy on us;
you are seated at the right hand of the Father:
receive our prayer.
For you alone are the Holy One,
you alone are the Lord,
you alone are the Most High,
Jesus Christ,
with the Holy Spirit,
in the glory of God the Father. Amen.

OPENING PRAYER

Afterwards the priest, with hands joined, sings or says:

Let us pray.

Priest and people pray silently for a while.
Then the priest extends his hands and sings or says the opening prayer:
at the end of which the people respond:

℟. Amen.

A

Father,
you have made the bond of marriage
a holy mystery,
a symbol of Christ's love for his Church.
Hear our prayers for N. **and** N.
With faith in you and in each other
they pledge their love today.
May their lives always bear witness
to the reality of that love.

We ask this
through our Lord Jesus Christ, your Son,
who lives and reigns with you and the Holy Spirit,
one God, for ever and ever. ℟. Amen.

B

Father,
hear our prayers for N. **and** N.
who today are united in marriage before your altar.
Give them your blessing, and strengthen their love for each other.

We ask this
through our Lord Jesus Christ, your Son,
who lives and reigns with you and the Holy Spirit,
one God, for ever and ever. ℟. Amen.

C

Almighty God,
hear our prayers for N. **and** N.,
who have come here today
to be united in the sacrament of marriage.
Increase their faith in you and in each other,
and through them bless your Church (**with Christian children**).

We ask this
through our Lord Jesus Christ, your Son,
who lives and reigns with you and the Holy Spirit,
one God, for ever and ever. ℟. Amen.

D

Father,
when you created mankind
you willed that man and wife should be one.
Bind N. **and** N.
in the loving union of marriage;
and make their love fruitful so that they may be living witnesses
to your divine love in the world.

We ask this
through our Lord Jesus Christ, your Son,
who lives and reigns with you and the Holy Spirit,
one God, for ever and ever. ℟. Amen.

LITURGY OF THE WORD

21. The liturgy of the word is celebrated according to the rubrics. There may be three readings, the first of them from the Old Testament.

The reader goes to the lectern for the first reading. All sit and listen.

(See p. 139 for a short summary and evaluation of each Old Testament reading.)

To indicate the end, the reader adds:

This is the Word of the Lord.

All respond:

Thanks be to God.

The cantor of the psalm sings or recites the psalm, and the people make the response.

If there is a second reading, it is read at the lectern as before.

To indicate the end, the reader adds:

This is the Word of the Lord.

All respond:

Thanks be to God.

The **alleluia** or other chant follows.

Meanwhile, if incense is used, the priest puts some in the censer. Then the deacon who is to proclaim the gospel bows before the priest and in a low voice asks the blessing:

Father, give me your blessing.

The priest says in a low voice:

The Lord be in your heart and on your lips
that you may worthily proclaim his gospel.

In the name of the Father, and of the Son, ✠ and of the Holy Spirit.

The deacon answers:

Amen.

If there is no deacon, the priest bows before the altar and says quietly:

**Almighty God, cleanse my heart and my lips
that I may worthily proclaim your gospel.**

Then the deacon (or the priest) goes to the lectern. He may be accompanied by ministers with incense and candles. He sings or says:

The Lord be with you.

The people answer:

And also with you.

The deacon (or priest) sings or says:

A reading from the holy gospel according to N.

He makes the sign of the cross on the book, and then on his forehead, lips, and breast.

The people respond:

Glory to you, Lord.

Then, if incense is used, the deacon (or priest) incenses the book and proclaims the gospel.

At the end of the gospel, the deacon (or priest) adds:

This is the gospel of the Lord.

All respond:

Praise to you, Lord Jesus Christ.

Then he kisses the book, saying quietly:

May the words of the gospel wipe away our sins.

HOMILY

After the gospel, the priest gives a homily drawn from the sacred text. He speaks about the mystery of Christian marriage, the dignity of wedded love, the grace of the sacrament and the responsibilities of married people, keeping in mind the circumstances of this particular marriage.

RITE OF MARRIAGE

All stand, including the bride and the bridegroom and the priest addresses them in these or similar words:

My dear friends, you have come together in this church so that the Lord may seal and strengthen your love in the presence of the Church's minister and this community. Christ abundantly blesses this love. He has already consecrated you in baptism and now he enriches and strengthens you by a special sacrament so that you may assume the duties of marriage in mutual and lasting fidelity. And so, in the presence of the Church, I ask you to state your intentions.

The priest tnen questions them about their freedom of choice, faithfulness to each other, and the acceptance and upbringing of children:

N. and N., have you come here freely and without reservation to give yourselves to each other in marriage?
Will you love and honor each other as man and wife for the rest of your lives?

The following question may be omitted if, for example, the couple is advanced in years.

Will you accept children lovingly from God, and bring them up according to the law of Christ and his Church?

Each answers the questions separately.

CONSENT

The priest invites the couple to declare their consent:

Since it is your intention to enter into marriage, join your right hands, and declare your consent before God and his Church.

They join hands.

The bridegroom says:

A I, N., take you, N., to be my wife. I promise to be true to you in good times and in bad, in sickness and in health. I will love you and honor you all the days of my life.

The bride says:

I, N., take you, N., to be my husband. I promise to be true to you in good times and in bad, in sickness and in health. I will love you and honor you all the days of my life.

In the dioceses of the United States the following form may be used:

The bridegroom says:

B **I, N., take you, N., for my lawful wife, to have and to hold, from this day forward, for better, for worse, for richer, for poorer, in sickness and in health, until death do us part.**

The bride says:

I, N., take you, N., for my lawful husband, to have and to hold, from this day forward, for better, for worse, for richer, for poorer, in sickness and in health, until death do us part.

If, however, it seems preferable for pastoral reasons, the priest may obtain consent from the couple through questions.

First he asks the bridegroom:

A **N., do you take N. to be your wife? Do you promise to be true to her in good times and in bad, in sickness and in health, to love her and honor her all the days of your life?**

The bridegroom: **I do.**

Then he asks the bride:

N., do you take N. to be your husband? Do you promise to be true to him in good times and in bad, in sickness and in health, to love him and honor him all the days of your life?

The bride: **I do.**

In dioceses of the United States the following form may be used:

First he asks the bridegroom:

B **N., do you take N. for your lawful wife, to have and to hold, from this day forward, for better, for worse, for richer, for poorer, in sickness and in health, until death do you part?**

The bridegroom: **I do.**

Then he asks the bride:

N., do you take N. for your lawful husband, to have and to hold, from this day forward, for better, for worse, for richer, for poorer, in sickness and in health, until death do you part?

The bride: **I do.**

If pastoral necessity demands it, the conference of bishops may decree, in virtue of the faculty in no. 17, that the priest should always obtain the consent of the couple through questions.

Receiving their consent, the priest says:

You have declared your consent before the Church. May the Lord in his goodness strengthen your consent and fill you both with his blessings.
What God has joined, men must not divide.

℟. Amen.

BLESSING AND EXCHANGE OF RINGS

Priest:

1

May the Lord bless ✠ these rings
which you give to each other
as the sign of your love and fidelity.

℟. Amen.

2

Lord, bless these rings which we bless ✠ in your name.
Grant that those who wear them
may always have a deep faith in each other.
May they do your will
and always live together
in peace, good will, and love.
We ask this through Christ our Lord.

℟. Amen.

3

Lord,
bless ✠ and consecrate N. **and** N.
in their love for each other.
May these rings be a symbol
of true faith in each other,
and always remind them of their love.
Through Christ our Lord. ℟. Amen.

The bridegroom places his wife's ring on her ring finger.
He may say:

N., take this ring as a sign of my love and fidelity. In the name of the Father, and of the Son, and of the Holy Spirit.

The bride places her husband's ring on his ring finger. She may say:

N., take this ring as a sign of my love and fidelity. In the name of the Father, and of the Son, and of the Holy Spirit.

GENERAL INTERCESSIONS

The general intercessions (prayer of the faithful) follow, using formulas approved by the conference of bishops.

PROFESSION OF FAITH

If the rubrics call for it, the profession of faith is said after the general intercessions.

We believe in one God,
the Father, the Almighty,
maker of heaven and earth,
of all that is seen and unseen.

We believe in one Lord, Jesus Christ,
the only Son of God,
eternally begotten of the Father,
God from God, Light from Light,
true God from true God,
begotten, not made, one in Being with the Father.
Through him all things were made.
For us men and for our salvation
he came down from heaven:

All bow at the following words up to: **and became man.**

by the power of the Holy Spirit
he was born of the Virgin Mary, and became man.

For our sake he was crucified under Pontius Pilate;
he suffered, died, and was buried.
On the third day he rose again
in fulfillment of the Scriptures;
he ascended into heaven
and is seated at the right hand of the Father.
He will come again in glory to judge the living and the dead,
and his kingdom will have no end.

We believe in the Holy Spirit, the Lord, the giver of life,
who proceeds from the Father and the Son.
With the Father and the Son he is worshiped and glorified.
He has spoken through the Prophets.
We believe in one holy catholic and apostolic Church.
We acknowledge one baptism for the forgiveness of sins.
We look for the resurrection of the dead,
and the life of the world to come. Amen.

THE LITURGY OF THE EUCHARIST

After the liturgy of the word, the offertory song is begun.

Meanwhile the ministers place the corporal, the purificator, the chalice, and the missal on the altar.

It is desirable that the participation of the faithful be expressed by members of the congregation bringing up the bread and wine for the celebration of the eucharist or other gifts for the needs of the Church and the poor. During the offertory, the bride and bridegroom may bring the bread and wine to the altar.

The priest, standing at the altar, takes the paten with the bread and, holding it slightly raised above the altar, says quietly:

**Blessed are you, Lord, God of all creation.
Through your goodness we have this bread to offer,
which earth has given and human hands have made.
It will become for us the bread of life.**

Then he places the paten with the bread on the corporal.

If no offertory song is sung, the priest may say the preceding words in an audible voice; then the people may respond:

Blessed be God for ever.

The deacon (or the priest) pours wine and a little water into the chalice, saying quietly:

**By the mystery of this water and wine
may we come to share in the divinity of Christ,
who humbled himself to share in our humanity.**

Then the priest takes the chalice and holding it slightly raised above the altar, says quietly:

**Blessed are you, Lord, God of all creation.
Through your goodness we have this wine to offer,
fruit of the vine and work of human hands.
It will become our spiritual drink.**

Then he places the chalice on the corporal.

If no offertory song is sung, the priest may say the preceding words in an audible voice; then the people may respond:

Blessed be God for ever.

The priest bows and says quietly:

Lord God, we ask you to receive us
and be pleased with the sacrifice we offer you
with humble and contrite hearts.

He may now incense the offerings and the altar. Afterwards the deacon or a minister incenses the priest and people.

Next the priest stands at the side of the altar and washes his hands, saying quietly:

Lord, wash away my iniquity;
cleanse me from my sin.

Standing at the center of the altar, facing the people, he extends and then joins his hands, saying:

Pray, brethren, that our sacrifice
may be acceptable to God, the almighty Father.

The people answer:

May the Lord accept the sacrifice at your hands
for the praise and glory of his name,
for our good, and the good of all his Church.

PRAYER OVER THE GIFTS

With hands extended, the priest sings or says one of the following:

A

Lord,
accept our offering
for this newly-married couple, N. and N.
By your love and providence you have brought them together;
now bless them all the days of their married life.
(We ask this) through Christ our Lord.

℟. Amen.

B

Lord,
accept the gifts we offer you
on this happy day.
In your fatherly love
watch over and protect N. and N.,
whom you have united in marriage.
(We ask this) through Christ our Lord.

℟. Amen.

C

Lord,
hear our prayers
and accept the gifts we offer for N. and N.
Today you have made them one in the sacrament of marriage.
May the mystery of Christ's unselfish love,
which we celebrate in this eucharist,
increase their love for you and for each other.
(We ask this) through Christ our Lord.

℟. Amen.

THE EUCHARISTIC PRAYER

The priest begins the eucharistic prayer. With hands extended, he sings or says:

The Lord be with you.

The people answer:

And also with you.

He lifts up his hands and continues:

Lift up your hearts.

The people:

We lift them up to the Lord.

With hands extended, he continues:

Let us give thanks to the Lord our God.

The people:

It is right to give him thanks and praise.

The priest continues the preface with hands extended.

At the end of the preface he joins his hands and, together with the people, concludes it by singing or saying aloud:

Holy, holy, holy Lord, God of power and might,
heaven and earth are full of your glory.
Hosanna in the highest.
Blessed is he who comes in the name of the Lord.
Hosanna in the highest.

In all Masses the priest may say the eucharistic prayer in an audible voice. In sung Masses he may sing those parts of the eucharistic prayer which may be sung in a concelebrated Mass.

In the first eucharistic prayer (the Roman canon) the words in parentheses may be omitted.

PREFACE

A

℣. **The Lord be with you.**

℟. And also with you.

℣. **Lift up your hearts.**

℟. We lift them up to the Lord.

℣. **Let us give thanks to the Lord our God.**

℟. It is right to give him thanks and praise.

**Father, all-powerful and ever-living God,
we do well always and everywhere to give you thanks.
By this sacrament your grace unites man and woman
in an unbreakable bond of love and peace.**

**You have designed the chaste love of husband and wife
for the increase both of the human family
and of your own family born in baptism.**

**You are the loving Father of the world of nature;
you are the loving Father of the new creation of grace.
In Christian marriage you bring together the two orders of creation:
nature's gift of children enriches the world
and your grace enriches also your Church.**

**Through Christ the choirs of angels
and all the saints
praise and worship your glory.
May our voices blend with theirs
as we join in their unending hymn:**

**Holy, holy, holy Lord, God of power and might,
heaven and earth are full of your glory.
Hosanna in the highest.
Blessed is he who comes in the name of the Lord.
Hosanna in the highest.**

B

℣. **The Lord be with you.**
℟. And also with you.
℣. **Lift up your hearts.**
℟. We lift them up to the Lord.
℣. **Let us give thanks to the Lord our God.**
℟. It is right to give him thanks and praise.

Father, all-powerful and ever-living God,
we do well always and everywhere to give you thanks
through Jesus Christ our Lord.

Through him you entered into a new covenant with your people.
You restored man to grace in the saving mystery of redemption.
You gave him a share in the divine life
through his union with Christ.
You made him an heir of Christ's eternal glory.

This outpouring of love in the new covenant of grace
is symbolized in the marriage covenant
that seals the love of husband and wife
and reflects your divine plan of love.

And so, with the angels and all the saints in heaven
we proclaim your glory
and join in their unending hymn of praise:

Holy, holy, holy Lord, God of power and might,
heaven and earth are full of your glory.
Hosanna in the highest.
Blessed is he who comes in the name of the Lord.
Hosanna in the highest.

C

℣. **The Lord be with you.**

℟. And also with you.

℣. **Lift up your hearts.**

℟. We lift them up to the Lord.

℣. **Let us give thanks to the Lord our God.**

℟. It is right to give him thanks and praise.

Father, all-powerful and ever-living God,
we do well always and everywhere to give you thanks.
You created man in love to share your divine life.
We see his high destiny in the love of husband and wife,
which bears the imprint of your own divine love.

Love is man's origin,
love is his constant calling,
love is his fulfillment in heaven.

The love of man and woman
is made holy in the sacrament of marriage,
and becomes the mirror of your everlasting love.
Through Christ the choirs of angels
and all the saints
praise and worship your glory.
May our voices blend with theirs
as we join in their unending hymn:

Holy, holy, holy Lord, God of power and might,
heaven and earth are full of your glory.
Hosanna in the highest.
Blessed is he who comes in the name of the Lord.
Hosanna in the highest.

EUCHARISTIC PRAYER I

THE ROMAN CANON

1

The priest, with hands extended, says:

**We come to you, Father,
with praise and thanksgiving,
through Jesus Christ your Son.**

He joins his hands and, making the sign of the cross once over both bread and chalice, says:

**Through him we ask you to accept and bless ✠
these gifts we offer you in sacrifice.**

With hands extended, he continues:

**We offer them for your holy catholic Church,
watch over it, Lord, and guide it;
grant it peace and unity throughout the world.
We offer them for N. our Pope,
for N. our bishop,
and for all who hold and teach the catholic faith
that comes to us from the apostles.**

Commemoration of the living.

**Remember, Lord, your people,
especially those for whom we now pray, N. and N.**

He prays for them briefly with hands joined. Then, with hands extended, he continues:

**Remember all of us gathered here before you.
You know how firmly we believe in you
and dedicate ourselves to you.
We offer you this sacrifice of praise
for ourselves and those who are dear to us.
We pray to you, our living and true God,
for our well-being and redemption.**

1 **Within the Action.**

In union with the whole Church
we honor Mary,
the ever-virgin mother of Jesus Christ our Lord and God.
We honor Joseph, her husband,
the apostles and martyrs
Peter and Paul, Andrew,
(James, John, Thomas,
James, Philip,
Bartholomew, Matthew, Simon and Jude;
we honor Linus, Cletus, Clement, Sixtus,
Cornelius, Cyprian, Lawrence, Chrysogonus,
John and Paul, Cosmas and Damian)

SPECIAL COMMUNICANTES

Christmas and during the octave

In union with the whole Church
we celebrate that day (night)
when Mary without loss of her virginity
gave this world its savior.
We honor her . . .

Epiphany

In union with the whole Church
we celebrate that day
when your only Son,
sharing your eternal glory,
showed himself in a human body.
We honor Mary . . .

From the Easter Vigil to the Saturday before the Second Sunday of Easter inclusive:

In union with the whole Church
we celebrate that day (night)
when Jesus Christ, our Lord,
rose from the dead in his human body.
We honor Mary . . .

and all the saints.
May their merits and prayers
gain us your constant help and protection.
(Through Christ our Lord. Amen.) 1

With hands extended, he continues:

Father, accept this offering
from your whole family
and from N. and N., for whom we now pray.
You have brought them to their wedding day:
grant them (the gift and joy of children and)
a long and happy life together.

He joins his hands.

(Through Christ our Lord. Amen.)

With hands outstretched over the offerings, he says:

Bless and approve our offering;
make it acceptable to you,
an offering in spirit and in truth.
Let it become for us
the body and blood of Jesus Christ,
your only Son, our Lord.

He joins his hands.

SPECIAL COMMUNICANTES

In union with the whole Church
we celebrate that day
when your only Son, our Lord,
took his place with you
and raised our frail human nature to glory.
We honor Mary . . .

Pentecost

In union with the whole Church
we celebrate the day of Pentecost
when the Holy Spirit appeared to the apostles
in the form of countless tongues.
We honor Mary . . .

1 The words of the Lord in the following formulas should be spoken clearly and distinctly, as their meaning demands.

The day before he suffered

He takes the bread and, raising it a little above the altar, continues:

he took bread in his sacred hands

He looks upward.

and looking up to heaven,
to you, his almighty Father,
he gave you thanks and praise.
He broke the bread,
gave it to his disciples, and said:

He bows slightly.

Take this, all of you, and eat it:
this is my body which will be given up for you.

He shows the consecrated host to the people, places it on the paten, and genuflects in adoration.

Then he continues:

When supper was ended,

He takes the chalice and, raising it a little above the altar, continues:

he took the cup.
Again he gave you thanks and praise,
gave the cup to his disciples, and said:

He bows slightly.

Take this, all of you, and drink from it:
this is the cup of my blood,
the blood of the new and everlasting covenant.
It will be shed for you and for all men
so that sins may be forgiven.
Do this in memory of me.

He shows the chalice to the people, places it on the corporal, and genuflects in adoration.

Then he sings or says:

Let us proclaim the mystery of faith:

And the people take up the acclamation:

(a) Christ has died,
Christ is risen,
Christ will come again.

(b) Dying you destroyed our death,
rising you restored our life.
Lord Jesus, come in glory.

(c) When we eat this bread and drink this cup,
we proclaim your death, Lord Jesus,
until you come in glory.

(d) Lord, by your cross and resurrection
you have set us free.
You are the Savior of the world.

Then, with hands extended, the priest says:

**Father, we celebrate the memory of Christ, your Son.
We, your people and your ministers,
recall his passion,
his resurrection from the dead,
and his ascension into glory;
and from the many gifts you have given us
we offer to you, God of glory and majesty,
this holy and perfect sacrifice:
the bread of life
and the cup of eternal salvation.**

**Look with favor on these offerings
and accept them as once you accepted
the gifts of your servant Abel,
the sacrifice of Abraham, our father in faith,
and the bread and wine offered by your priest Melchisedech.**

Bowing, with hands joined, he continues:

1 **Almighty God,**
we pray that your angel may take this sacrifice
to your altar in heaven.
Then, as we receive from this altar
the sacred body and blood of your Son,

He stands up straight and makes the sign of the cross, saying:

let us be filled with every grace and blessing.

He joins his hands.

(Through Christ our Lord. Amen.)

Commemoration of the dead.

With hands extended, he says:

Remember, Lord, those who have died
and have gone before us marked with the sign of faith,
especially those for whom we now pray, N. and N.

The priest prays for them briefly with joined hands. Then, with hands extended, he continues:

May these, and all who sleep in Christ,
find in your presence
light, happiness, and peace.

He joins his hands.

(Through Christ our Lord. Amen.)

With hands extended, he continues:

For ourselves, too, we ask
some share in the fellowship of your apostles and martyrs,
with John the Baptist, Stephen, Matthias, Barnabas,
(Ignatius, Alexander, Marcellinus, Peter,
Felicity, Perpetua, Agatha, Lucy,
Agnes, Cecilia, Anastasia)
and all the saints.

The celebrant strikes his breast with the right hand, saying:

Though we are sinners,
we trust in your mercy and love.

With his hands extended as before, he continues:

Do not consider what we truly deserve,
but grant us your forgiveness.

He joins his hands and continues:

Through Christ our Lord
you give us all these gifts.
You fill them with life and goodness,
you bless them and make them holy.

He takes the chalice and the paten with the host and, lifting them up, says:

Through him,
with him,
in him,
in the unity of the Holy Spirit,
all glory and honor is yours,
almighty Father,
for ever and ever.

The people respond:

Amen.

EUCHARISTIC PRAYER II

℣. The Lord be with you.

℟. And also with you.

℣. Lift up your hearts.

℟. We lift them up to the Lord.

℣. Let us give thanks to the Lord our God.

℟. It is right to give him thanks and praise.

72. **Father, it is our duty and our salvation,
always and everywhere
to give you thanks
through your beloved Son, Jesus Christ.
He is the Word through whom you made the universe,
the Savior you sent to redeem us.
By the power of the Holy Spirit
he took flesh and was born of the Virgin Mary.
For our sake he opened his arms on the cross;
he put an end to death
and revealed the resurrection.
In this he fulfilled your will
and won for you a holy people.
And so we join the angels and the saints
in proclaiming your glory
as we sing (say):**

**Holy, holy, holy Lord, God of power and might,
heaven and earth are full of your glory.
Hosanna in the highest.
Blessed is he who comes in the name of the Lord.
Hosanna in the highest.**

The priest, with hands extended, says:

**Lord, you are holy indeed,
the fountain of all holiness.**

He joins his hands and, holding them outstretched over the offerings, says:

**Let your Spirit come upon these gifts to make them holy,
so that they may become for us**

He joins his hands and, making the sign of the cross once over both bread and chalice, says:

the body ✠ and blood of our Lord, Jesus Christ.

He joins his hands.

The words of the Lord in the following formulas should be spoken clearly and distinctly, as their meaning demands.

**Before he was given up to death,
a death he freely accepted,**

He takes the bread and, raising it a little above the altar, continues:

**he took bread and gave you thanks.
He broke the bread,
gave it to his disciples, and said:**

He bows slightly.

**Take this, all of you, and eat it:
this is my body which will be given up for you.**

He shows the consecrated host to the people, places it on the paten, and genuflects in adoration.
Then he continues:

When supper was ended, he took the cup.

He takes the chalice and, raising it a little above the altar, continues:

**Again he gave you thanks and praise,
gave the cup to his disciples, and said:**

He bows slightly.

**Take this, all of you, and drink from it:
this is the cup of my blood,
the blood of the new and everlasting covenant.
It will be shed for you and for all men
so that sins may be forgiven.
Do this in memory of me.**

2 He shows the chalice to the people, places it on the corporal, and genuflects in adoration.

Then he sings or says:

Let us proclaim the mystery of faith:

And the people take up the acclamation:

(a) Christ has died,
Christ is risen,
Christ will come again.

Other acclamations

(b) Dying you destroyed our death,
rising you restored our life.
Lord Jesus, come in glory.

(c) When we eat this bread and drink this cup,
we proclaim your death, Lord Jesus,
until you come in glory.

(d) Lord, by your cross and resurrection
you have set us free.
You are the Savior of the world.

With hands extended, the priest says:

In memory of his death and resurrection,
we offer you, Father, this life-giving bread,
this saving cup.

We thank you for counting us worthy
to stand in your presence and serve you.
May all of us who share in the body and blood of Christ
be brought together in unity by the Holy Spirit.
Lord, remember your Church throughout the world;
make us grow in love,
together with N. our Pope,
N. our bishop, and all the clergy.

Remember our brothers and sisters **2**
who have gone to their rest
in the hope of rising again;
bring them and all the departed
into the light of your presence.
Have mercy on us all;
make us worthy to share eternal life
with Mary, the virgin mother of God,
with the apostles,
and with all the saints who have done your will throughout the ages.
May we praise you in union with them,
and give you glory

He joins his hands.

through your Son, Jesus Christ.

He takes the chalice and the paten with the host and, lifting them up, says:

Through him,
with him,
in him,
in the unity of the Holy Spirit,
all glory and honor is yours,
almighty Father,
for ever and ever.

The people respond:

Amen.

3

EUCHARISTIC PRAYER III

The priest, with hands extended, says:

**Father, you are holy indeed,
and all creation rightly gives you praise.
All life, all holiness comes from you
through your Son, Jesus Christ our Lord,
by the working of the Holy Spirit.
From age to age you gather a people to yourself,
so that from east to west
a perfect offering may be made
to the glory of your name.**

He joins his hands and, holding them outstretched over the offerings, says:

**And so, Father, we bring you these gifts.
We ask you to make them holy by the power of your Spirit,**

He joins his hands and, making the sign of the cross once over both bread and chalice, says:

**that they may become the body ✠ and blood
of your Son, our Lord Jesus Christ,
at whose command we celebrate this eucharist.**

He joins his hands.

The words of the Lord in the following formulas should be spoken clearly and distinctly, as their meaning demands.

On the night he was betrayed,

He takes the bread and, raising it a little above the altar, continues:

**He took bread and gave you thanks and praise.
He broke the bread, gave it to his disciples, and said:**

He bows slightly.

**Take this, all of you, and eat it:
this is my body which will be given up for you.**

He shows the consecrated host to the people, places it on the paten, and genuflects in adoration.

Then he continues:

When supper was ended, he took the cup.

He takes the chalice and, raising it a little above the altar, continues:

Again he gave you thanks and praise,
gave the cup to his disciples, and said:

He bows slightly.

Take this, all of you, and drink from it:
this is the cup of my blood,
the blood of the new and everlasting covenant.
It will be shed for you and for all men
so that sins may be forgiven.
Do this in memory of me.

He shows the chalice to the people, places it on the corporal, and genuflects in adoration.

Then he sings or says:

Let us proclaim the mystery of faith:

The people continue the acclamation:

(a) Christ has died,
Christ is risen,
Christ will come again.

(b) Dying you destroyed our death,
rising you restored our life.
Lord Jesus, come in glory.

(c) When we eat this bread and drink this cup,
we proclaim your death, Lord Jesus,
until you come in glory.

(d) Lord, by your cross and resurrection
you have set us free.
You are the Savior of the world.

With hands extended, the priest says:

3 **Father, calling to mind the death your Son endured for our salvation,**
his glorious resurrection and ascension into heaven,
and ready to greet him when he comes again,
we offer you in thanksgiving this holy and living sacrifice.

Look with favor on your Church's offering.
and see the Victim whose death has reconciled us to yourself.
Grant that we, who are nourished by his body and blood,
may be filled with his Holy Spirit,
and become one body, one spirit in Christ.

May he make us an everlasting gift to you
and enable us to share in the inheritance of your saints,
with Mary, the virgin mother of God;
with the apostles, the martyrs,
(Saint N.—the saint of the day or the patron saint) **and all your saints,**
on whose constant intercession we rely for help.

Lord, may this sacrifice, which has made our peace with you,
advance the peace and salvation of all the world.
Strengthen in faith and love your pilgrim Church on earth;
your servant, Pope N.**, our bishop** N.**,**
and all the bishops,
with the clergy and the entire people your Son has gained for you.

Father, hear the prayers of the family you have gathered here before you. 3
In mercy and love unite all your children
wherever they may be.
Welcome into your kingdom our departed brothers and sisters,
and all who have left this world in your friendship.

He joins his hands.

We hope to enjoy for ever the vision of your glory,
through Christ our Lord, from whom all good things come.

He takes the chalice and the paten with the host and, lifting them ur

Through him,
with him,
in him,
in the unity of the Holy Spirit,
all glory and honor is yours,
almighty Father,
for ever and ever.

The people respond:

Amen.

EUCHARISTIC PRAYER IV

4

℣. The Lord be with you.

℟. And also with you.

℣. Lift up your hearts.

℟. We lift them up to the Lord.

℣. Let us give thanks to the Lord our God.

℟. It is right to give him thanks and praise.

Father in heaven, it is right that we should give you thanks and glory:
you alone are God, living and true.
Through all eternity you live in unapproachable light.
Source of life and goodness, you have created all things,
to fill your creatures with every blessing
and lead all men to the joyful vision of your light.
Countless hosts of angels stand before you to do your will;
they look upon your splendor
and praise you, night and day.
United with them, and in the name of every creature under heaven,
we too praise your glory as we sing (say):

Holy, holy, holy Lord, God of power and might,
heaven and earth are full of your glory.
Hosanna in the highest.
Blessed is he who comes in the name of the Lord.
Hosanna in the highest.

The priest, with hands extended, says:

Father, we acknowledge your greatness:
all your actions show your wisdom and love.

You formed man in your own likeness
and set him over the whole world
to serve you, his creator,
and to rule over all creatures.
Even when he disobeyed you and lost your friendship
you did not abandon him to the power of death,
but helped all men to seek and find you.
Again and again you offered a covenant to man,
and through the prophets taught him to hope for salvation.
Father, you so loved the world
that in the fullness of time you sent your only Son to be our Savior.
He was conceived through the power of the Holy Spirit, and born of the Virgin Mary,
a man like us in all things but sin.
To the poor he proclaimed the good news of salvation,
to prisoners, freedom,
and to those in sorrow, joy.
In fulfillment of your will
he gave himself up to death;
but by rising from the dead,
he destroyed death and restored life.
And that we might live no longer for ourselves but for him,
he sent the Holy Spirit from you, Father,
as his first gift to those who believe,
to complete his work on earth
and bring us the fullness of grace.

4 He joins his hands and, holding them outstretched over the offerings, says:

Father, may this Holy Spirit sanctify these offerings.

He joins his hands and, making the sign of the cross once over both bread and chalice, says:

Let them become the body ✠ and blood of Jesus Christ our Lord

He joins his hands.

as we celebrate the great mystery
which he left us as an everlasting covenant.

The words of the Lord in the following formulas should be spoken clearly and distinctly, as their meaning demands.

He always loved those who were his own in the world.
When the time came for him to be glorified by you, his heavenly Father,
he showed the depth of his love.
While they were at supper,

He takes the bread and, raising it a little above the altar, continues:

he took bread, said the blessing, broke the bread
and gave it to his disciples, saying:

He bows slightly.

Take this, all of you, and eat it:
this is my body which will be given up for you.

He shows the consecrated host to the people, places it on the paten, and genuflects in adoration.

Then he continues:

In the same way, he took the cup, filled with wine.

He takes the chalice and, raising it a little above the altar, continues:

He gave you thanks, and giving the cup to his disciples, said: 4

He bows slightly.

Take this, all of you, and drink from it:
this is the cup of my blood,
the blood of the new and everlasting covenant.
It will be shed for you and for all men
so that sins may be forgiven.
Do this in memory of me.

He shows the chalice to the people, places it on the corporal, and genuflects in adoration.

Then he sings or says:

Let us proclaim the mystery of faith:

And the people take up the acclamation:

(a) Christ has died,
Christ is risen,
Christ will come again.

(b) Dying you destroyed our death,
rising you restored our life.
Lord Jesus, come in glory.

(c) When we eat this bread and drink this cup,
we proclaim your death, Lord Jesus,
until you come in glory.

(d) Lord, by your cross and resurrection
you have set us free.
You are the Savior of the world.

With hands extended, the priest says:

Father, we now celebrate this memorial of our redemption.
We recall Christ's death, his descent among the dead,
his resurrection, and his ascension to your right hand;
and, looking forward to his coming in glory, we offer you his body and blood,
the acceptable sacrifice which brings salvation to the whole world.

4 Lord, look upon this sacrifice which you have given to your Church;
and by your Holy Spirit, gather all who share this bread and wine
into the one body of Christ, a living sacrifice of praise.

Lord, remember those for whom we offer this sacrifice,
especially N. our Pope,
N. our bishop, and bishops and clergy everywhere.
Remember those who take part in this offering,
those here present and all your people,
and all who seek you with a sincere heart.
Remember those who have died in the peace of Christ
and all the dead whose faith is known to you alone.
Father, in your mercy grant also to us, your children,
to enter into our heavenly inheritance
in the company of the Virgin Mary, the mother of God,
and your apostles and saints.
Then, in your kingdom, freed from the corruption of sin and death,
we shall sing your glory with every creature through Christ our Lord,

He joins his hands.

through whom you give us everything that is good.

He takes the chalice and the paten with the host and, lifting them up, says:

Through him,
with him,
in him,
in the unity of the Holy Spirit,
all glory and honor is yours,
almighty Father,
for ever and ever. The people respond: **Amen.**

COMMUNION RITE

The priest sets down the chalice and paten and, with hands joined, sings or says:

**Let us pray with confidence to the Father
in the words our Savior gave us:**

THE LORD'S PRAYER

He extends his hands and continues, with the people:

**Our Father, who art in heaven,
hallowed be thy name;
thy kingdom come;
thy will be done on earth as it is in heaven.
Give us this day our daily bread;
and forgive us our trespasses
as we forgive those who trespass against us;
and lead us not into temptation,
but deliver us from evil.**

After the Lord's Prayer, the prayer **Deliver us** is omitted.

The priest faces the bride and bridegroom and, with hands joined, says one of the following forms:

(If one or both of the parties will not be receiving communion, the words in the introduction to the nuptial blessing, through the sacrament of the body and blood of Christ, may be omitted.)

NUPTIAL BLESSING

A

**My dear friends, let us turn to the Lord and pray
that he will bless with his grace this woman (or N.)
now married in Christ to this man (or N.)
and that (through the sacrament of the body and blood of Christ,)
he will unite in love the couple he has joined in this holy bond.**

All pray silently for a short while. Then the priest extends his hands and continues:

(If desired, in the prayer Father, by your power, two of the first three paragraphs may be omitted, keeping only the paragraphs which corresponds to the reading of the Mass.
In the last paragraph of this prayer, the words in parentheses may be omitted whenever circumstances suggest it, if, for example, the couple is advanced in years.)

**Father, by your power you have made everything out of nothing.
In the beginning you created the universe
and made mankind in your own likeness.
You gave man the constant help of woman
so that man and woman should no longer be two, but one flesh,
and you teach us that what you have united
may never be divided.**

**Father, you have made the union of man and wife so holy a mystery
that it symbolizes the marriage of Christ and his Church.**

**Father, by your plan man and woman are united,
and married life has been established
as the one blessing that was not forfeited by original sin
or washed away in the flood.**

Look with love upon this woman, your daughter,
now joined to her husband in marriage.
She asks your blessing.
Give her the grace of love and peace.
May she always follow the example of the holy women
whose praises are sung in the scriptures.

May her husband put his trust in her
and recognize that she is his equal
and the heir with him to the life of grace.
May he always honor her and love her
as Christ loves his bride, the Church.

Father, keep them always true to your commandments.
Keep them faithful in marriage
and let them be living examples of Christian life.
Give them the strength which comes from the gospel
so that they may be witnesses of Christ to others.
(Bless them with children
and help them to be good parents.
May they live to see their children's children.)
And, after a happy old age,
grant them fullness of life with the saints
in the kingdom of heaven.
We ask this through Christ our Lord.

℟. Amen.

B +

(b) In the following prayer, either the paragraph **Holy Father, you created mankind,** or the paragraph **Father, to reveal the plan of your love,** may be omitted, keeping only the paragraph which corresponds to the reading of the Mass.

Let us pray to the Lord for N. and N.
who come to God's altar at the beginning of their married life

**so that they may always be united in love for each other
(as now they share in the body and blood of Christ).**

All pray silently for a short while. Then the priest extends his hands and continues:

**Holy Father, you created mankind in your own image
and made man and woman to be joined as husband and wife
in union of body and heart
and so fulfill their mission in this world.**

**Father, to reveal the plan of your love,
you made the union of husband and wife
an image of the covenant between you and your people.
In the fulfillment of this sacrament,
the marriage of Christian man and woman
is a sign of the marriage between Christ and the Church.
Father, stretch out your hand, and bless** N. **and** N.

**Lord, grant that as they begin to live this sacrament
they may share with each other the gifts of your love
and become one in heart and mind
as witnesses to your presence in their marriage.
Help them to create a home together
(and give them children to be formed by the gospel
and to have a place in your family).**

Give your blessings to N.**, your daughter,
so that she may be a good wife (and mother),
caring for the home,
faithful in love for her husband,
generous and kind.
Give your blessings to** N.**, your son,
so that he may be a faithful husband
(and a good father.)**

Father, grant that as they come together to your table on earth, so they may one day have the joy of sharing your feast in heaven.
We ask this through Christ our Lord.
℟ Amen.

C

My dear friends, let us ask God
for his continued blessing upon this bridegroom and his bride (or N. and N.).

All pray silently for a short while. Then the priest extends his hands and continues:

Holy Father, creator of the universe,
maker of man and woman in your own likeness,
source of blessing for married life,
we humbly pray to you for this woman
who today is united with her husband in this sacrament of marriage.

May your fullest blessing come upon her and her husband
so that they may together rejoice in your gift of married love
(and enrich your Church with their children).

Lord, may they both praise you when they are happy
and turn to you in their sorrows.
May they be glad that you help them in their work
and know that you are with them in their need.
May they pray to you in the community of the Church,
and be your witnesses in the world.
May they reach old age in the company of their friends,
and come at last to the kingdom of heaven.
We ask this through Christ our Lord.
℟. Amen.

SIGN OF PEACE

Then the priest, with hands extended, says aloud:

Lord Jesus Christ, you said to your apostles:
I leave you peace, my peace I give you.
Look not on our sins, but on the faith of your Church,
and grant us the peace and unity of your kingdom

He joins his hands.

where you live for ever and ever.

The people answer:

℟. Amen.

The priest, extending and joining his hands, adds:

The peace of the Lord be with you always.

The people answer:

And also with you.

Then the deacon (or the priest) may add:

Let us offer each other the sign of peace.

The married couple and all present show their peace and love for one another in an appropriate way.

The priest gives the sign of peace to the deacon or the minister.

He then takes the host and breaks it over the paten. He places a small piece in the chalice, saying quietly:

May this mingling of the body and blood of our Lord Jesus Christ bring eternal life to us who receive it.

Meanwhile the following is sung or said:

Lamb of God, you take away the sins of the world:
have mercy on us.

Lamb of God, you take away the sins of the world:
have mercy on us.

Lamb of God, you take away the sins of the world:
grant us peace.

This may be repeated until the breaking of the bread is finished, but the last phrase is always **Grant us peace.**

Then the priest joins his hands and says quietly:

A

Lord Jesus Christ, Son of the living God,
by the will of the Father and the work of the Holy Spirit
your death brought life to the world.
By your holy body and blood
free me from all my sins and from every evil.
Keep me faithful to your teaching,
and never let me be parted from you.

B

Lord Jesus Christ,
with faith in your love and mercy
I eat your body and drink your blood.
Let it not bring me condemnation,
but health in mind and body.

The priest genuflects. Taking the host, he raises it slightly over the paten and, facing the people, says aloud:

This is the Lamb of God
who takes away the sins of the world.
Happy are those who are called to his supper.

He adds, once only, with the people:

Lord, I am not worthy to receive you,
but only say the word and I shall be healed.

Facing the altar, the priest says quietly:

May the body of Christ bring me to everlasting life.

He reverently consumes the body of Christ.
Then he takes the chalice and says quietly:

May the blood of Christ bring me to everlasting life.

He reverently drinks the blood of Christ.

After this he takes the paten or other vessel and goes to the communicants. He takes a host for each one, raises it a little, and shows it, saying:

The body of Christ.

The communicant answers:

Amen.

and receives communion.

When a deacon gives communion he does the same.

The married couple may receive communion under both kinds.

While the priest receives the body of Christ, the communion song is begun.

When the communion has been completed, the priest or deacon cleans the paten over the chalice and then the chalice itself.

Then the priest may return to the chair. A period of silence may now be observed, or a psalm or song of praise may be sung.

Then, standing at the chair or at the altar, the priest sings or says:

Let us pray.

Priest and people pray in silence for a while, unless a period of silence has already been observed. Then the priest extends his hands and sings or says the prayer after communion:

A PRAYER AFTER COMMUNION

Lord,
in your love
you have given us this eucharist
to unite us with one another and with you.
As you have made N. **and** N.
one in this sacrament of marriage
(**and in the sharing of the one bread and the one cup**),
so now make them one in love for each other.

We ask this through Christ our Lord.
℟. Amen.

B

Lord,
we who have shared the food of your table
pray for our friends N. **and** N.,
whom you have joined together in marriage.
Keep them close to you always.
May their love for each other
proclaim to all the world
their faith in you.

We ask this through Christ our Lord.
℟. Amen.

C

Almighty God,
may the sacrifice we have offered
and the eucharist we have shared
strengthen the love of N. **and** N.,
and give us all your fatherly aid.

We ask this through Christ our Lord.
℟. Amen.

CONCLUDING RITE

If there are any brief announcements, they are made at this time.

The dismissal follows. Facing the people, the priest extends his hands and sings or says:

The Lord be with you.

The people answer:

And also with you.

SOLEMN BLESSING

Before blessing the people at the end of Mass, the priest blesses the bride and bridegroom, using one of the forms below:

A

God the eternal Father keep you in love with each other,
so that the peace of Christ may stay with you
and be always in your home.

℟. Amen.

May (your children bless you,)
your friends console you
and all men live in peace with you.

℟. Amen.

May you always bear witness to the love of God in this world
so that the afflicted and the needy
will find in you generous friends,
and welcome you into the joys of heaven.

℟. Amen.

And may almighty God bless you all,
the Father, and the Son, ✠ and the Holy Spirit.

℟. Amen.

B

**May God, the almighty Father,
give you his joy
and bless you (in your children).**

℟. Amen.

**May the only Son of God have mercy on you
and help you in good times and in bad.**

℟. Amen.

**May the Holy Spirit of God
always fill your hearts with his love.**

℟. Amen.

**And may almighty God bless you all,
the Father, and the Son, ✠ and the Holy Spirit.**

℟. Amen.

C

**May the Lord Jesus, who was a guest at the wedding in Cana,
bless you and your families and friends.**

℟. Amen.

**May Jesus, who loved his Church to the end,
always fill your hearts with his love.**

℟. Amen.

**May he grant that, as you believe in his resurrection,
so you may wait for him in joy and hope.**

℟. Amen.

And may almighty God bless you all,
the Father, and the Son, ✠ and the Holy Spirit.

℟. Amen.

D In the United States

May almighty God, with his Word of blessing, unite your hearts in the never-ending bond of pure love.

℟. Amen.

May your children bring you happiness, and may your generous love for them be returned to you, many times over.

℟. Amen.

May the peace of Christ live always in your hearts and in your home.
May you have true friends to stand by you, both in joy and in sorrow.
May you be ready and willing to help and comfort all who come to you in need.
And may the blessings promised to the compassionate be yours in abundance.

℟. Amen.

May you find happiness and satisfaction in your work. May daily problems never cause you undue anxiety, nor the desire for earthly possessions dominate your lives. But may your hearts' first desire be always the good things waiting for you in the life of heaven.

℟. Amen.

May the Lord bless you with many happy years together, so that you may enjoy the rewards of a good life. And after you have

served him loyally in his kingdom on earth, may he welcome you to his eternal kingdom in heaven.

℟. Amen.

And may almighty God bless you all,
the Father, and the Son, ✠ and the Holy Spirit.

℟. Amen.

DISMISSAL

The deacon (or the priest), with hands joined, sings or says:

A

Go in the peace of Christ.

B

The Mass is ended, go in peace.

C

Go in peace to love and serve the Lord.

The people answer:

Thanks be to God.

The priest kisses the altar as at the beginning.

Then he makes the customary reverence with the ministers and leaves.

If any liturgical service follows immediately, the rite of dismissal is omitted.

If two or more marriages are celebrated at the same time, the questioning before the consent, the consent itself, and the acceptance of consent shall always be done individually for each couple; the rest, including the nuptial blessing, is said once for all, using the plural form.

CHAPTER V

TEXTS FOR USE IN THE MARRIAGE RITE AND IN THE WEDDING MASS

I. SCRIPTURE READINGS

In the wedding Mass and in marriages celebrated without Mass, the following selections may be used.

OLD TESTAMENT READING

67. Gn 1, 26-28. 31

1 **A reading from the book of Genesis**

Male and female he created them.

God said: "Let us make man in our image, after our likeness. Let them have dominion over the fish of the sea, the birds of the air, and the cattle, and over all the wild animals and all the creatures that crawl on the ground."

God created man in his image;
in the divine image he created him;
male and female he created them.

God blessed them, saying: "Be fertile and multiply; fill the earth and subdue it. Have dominion over the fish of the sea, the birds of the air, and all the living things that move on the earth." God looked at everything he had made, and he found it very good.

This is the Word of the Lord.

℟. Thanks be to God.

2

68. Gn 2:18-24

A reading from the book of Genesis

And they will be two in one flesh.

The Lord God said: "It is not good for the man to be alone. I will make a suitable partner for him." So the Lord God formed out of the ground various wild animals and various birds of the air, and he brought them to the man to see what he would call

them; whatever the man called each of them would be its name. The man gave names to all the cattle, all the birds of the air, and all the wild animals; but none proved to be the suitable partner for the man.

So the Lord God cast a deep sleep on the man, and while he was asleep, he took out one of his ribs and closed up its place with flesh. The Lord God then built up into a woman the rib that he had taken from the man. When he brought her to the man, the man said:

"This one, at last, is bone of my bones
and flesh of my flesh;
This one shall be called 'woman,'
for out of 'her man' this one has been taken."

That is why a man leaves his father and mother and clings to his wife, and the two of them become one body.

This is the Word of the Lord.

℟. Thanks be to God.

3 69. Gn 24, 48-51. 58-67

A reading from the book of Genesis

Isaac loved Rebekah, and so he was consoled for the loss of his mother.

The servant of Abraham said to Laban: "I bowed down in worship to the Lord, blessing the Lord, the God of my master Abraham, who had led me on the right road to obtain the daughter of my master's kinsman for his son. If, therefore, you have in mind to show true loyalty to my master, let me know; but if not, let me know that, too. I can then proceed accordingly."

Laban and his household said in reply: "This thing comes from the Lord; we can say nothing to you either for or against

it. Here is Rebekah, ready for you; take her with you, that she may become the wife of your master's son, as the Lord has said."

So they called Rebekah and asked her, "Do you wish to go with this man?" She answered, "I do." At this they allowed their sister Rebekah and her nurse to take leave, along with Abraham's servant and his men. Invoking a blessing on Rebekah, they said:

"Sister, may you grow
into thousands of myriads;
And may your descendants gain possession of the gates of their enemies!"

Then Rebekah and her maids started out; they mounted their camels and followed the man. So the servant took Rebekah and went on his way.

Meanwhile Isaac had gone from Beer-lahairoi and was living in the region of the Negeb. One day toward evening he went out . . . in the field, and as he looked around, he noticed that camels were approaching. Rebekah, too, was looking about and when she saw him, she alighted from her camel and asked the servant, "Who is the man out there, walking through the fields toward us?" "That is my master," replied the servant. Then she covered herself with her veil.

The servant recounted to Isaac all the things he had done. Then Isaac took Rebekah into his tent; he married her, and thus she became his wife. In his love for her Isaac found solace after the death of his mother Sarah.

This is the Word of the Lord.

℟. Thanks be to God.

4

70. Tb 7, 9-10. 11-15

A reading from the book of Tobit

May God join you together and fill you with his blessings.

Tobiah said to Raphael, "Brother Azariah, ask Raguel to let me marry my kinswoman Sarah." Raguel overheard the words; so he said to the boy: "Eat and drink and be merry tonight, for no man is more entitled to marry my daughter Sarah than you, brother. Besides, not even I have the right to give her to anyone but you, because you are my closest relative. But I will explain the situation to you very frankly. She is yours according to the decree of the Book of Moses. Your marriage to her has been decided in heaven! Take your kinswoman; from now on you are her love, and she is your beloved. She is yours today and ever after. And tonight, son, may the Lord of heaven prosper you both. May he grant you mercy and peace." Then Raguel called his daughter Sarah, and she came to him. He took her by the hand and gave her to Tobiah with the words: "Take her according to the law. According to the decree written in the Book of Moses she is your wife. Take her and bring her back safely to your father. And may the God of heaven grant both of you peace and prosperity." He then called her mother and told her to bring a scroll, so that he might draw up a marriage contract stating that he gave Sarah to Tobiah as his wife according to the decree of the Mosaic law. Her mother brought the scroll, and he drew up the contract, to which they affixed their seals.

Afterward they began to eat and drink.

This is the Word of the Lord.

℟. Thanks be to God.

5 71. 8, 5-7

A reading from the book of Tobit

May God bring us to old age together.

On the wedding night Sarah got up, and she and Tobiah started to pray and beg that deliverance might be theirs. He began with these words:

"Blessed are you, O God of our fathers;
praised be your name forever and ever.
Let the heavens and all your creation
praise you forever.
You made Adam and you gave him his wife Eve
to be his help and support;
and from these two the human race descended.
You said, 'It is not good for the man to be alone;
let us make him a partner like himself.'
Now, Lord, you know that I take this wife of mine
not because of lust,
but for a noble purpose.
Call down your mercy on me and on her,
and allow us to live together to a happy old age."

This is the Word of the Lord.
℟. Thanks be to God.

6 72. Sg 2, 8-10. 14. 16; 8, 6-7

A reading from the Song of Songs

For love is as strong as death.

Hark! my lover—here he comes
springing across the mountains,
leaping across the hills.
My lover is like a gazelle
or a young stag.

Here he stands behind our wall,
gazing through the windows,
peering through the lattices.
My lover speaks; he says to me,
"Arise, my beloved, my beautiful one,
and come!
"O my dove in the clefts of the rock,
in the secret recesses of the cliff,
Let me see you,
let me hear your voice,
For your voice is sweet,
and you are lovely."
My lover belongs to me and I to him.
[He said to me:]
Set me as a seal on your heart,
as a seal on your arm;
For stern as death is love,
relentless as the nether world is devotion;
its flames are a blazing fire.
Deep waters cannot quench love,
nor floods sweep it away.

This is the Word of the Lord.

℟. Thanks be to God.

7

73. Sir 26, 1-4. 13-16

A reading from the book of Sirach

Like the sun rising is the beauty of a good wife in a well-kept house.

Happy the husband of a good wife,
twice-lengthened are his days;
A worthy wife brings joy to her husband,
peaceful and full is his life.

A good wife is a generous gift
bestowed upon him who fears the Lord;
Be he rich or poor, his heart is content,
and a smile is ever on his face.
A gracious wife delights her husband,
her thoughtfulness puts flesh on his bones;
A gift from the Lord is her governed speech,
and her firm virtue is of surpassing worth.
Choicest of blessings is a modest wife,
priceless her chaste person.
Like the sun rising in the Lord's heavens,
the beauty of a virtuous wife is the radiance of her home.

This is the Word of the Lord.

℟. Thanks be to God.

8

74. Jer 31, 31-32. 33-34

A reading from the book of the prophet Jeremiah

I will make a new covenant with the house of Israel and Judah.

The days are coming, says the Lord, when I will make a new covenant with the house of Israel and the house of Judah. It will not be like the covenant I made with their fathers the day I took them by the hand to lead them forth from the land of Egypt. But this is the covenant which I will make with the house of Israel after those days, says the Lord. I will place my law within them, and write it upon their hearts; I will be their God, and they shall be my people. No longer will they have need to teach their friends and kinsmen how to know the Lord. All, from least to greatest, shall know me, says the Lord.

This is the Word of the Lord.

℟. Thanks be to God.

NEW TESTAMENT READING

1 75. Rom 8, 31-35. 37-39

A reading from the letter of Paul to the Romans

Who will separate us from the love of Christ?

If God is for us, who can be against us? Is it possible that he who did not spare his own Son but handed him over for the sake of us all will not grant us all things besides? Who shall bring a charge against God's chosen ones? God, who justifies? Who shall condemn them? Christ Jesus, who died or rather was raised up, who is at the right hand of God and who intercedes for us?

Who will separate us from the love of Christ? Trial, or distress, or persecution, or hunger, or nakedness, or danger, or the sword? Yet in all this we are more than conquerors because of him who has loved us. For I am certain that neither death nor life, neither angels nor principalities, neither the present nor the future, nor powers, neither height nor depth nor any other creature, will be able to separate us from the love of God that comes to us in Christ Jesus, our Lord.

This is the Word of the Lord.

℟. Thanks be to God.

2 76. Rom 12, 1-2. 9-18 or 12, 1-2. 9-13

A reading from the letter of Paul to the Romans

Offer to God your bodies as a living and holy sacrifice, truly pleasing to him.

(Long Form)

Brothers, I beg you through the mercy of God to offer your bodies as a living sacrifice holy and acceptable to God, your spiritual worship. Do not conform yourselves to this age but be

transformed by the renewal of your mind, so that you may judge what is God's will, what is good, pleasing and perfect.

Your love must be sincere. Detest what is evil, cling to what is good. Love one another with the affection of brothers. Anticipate each other in showing respect. Do not grow slack but be fervent in spirit; he whom you serve is the Lord. Rejoice in hope, be patient under trial, persevere in prayer. Look on the needs of the saints as your own; be generous in offering hospitality. Bless your persecutors; bless and do not curse them. Rejoice with those who rejoice, weep with those who weep. Have the same attitude toward all. Put away ambitious thoughts and associate with those who are lowly. Do not be wise in your own estimation. Never repay injury with injury. See that your conduct is honorable in the eyes of all. If possible, live peaceably with everyone.

This is the Word of the Lord.

℟. Thanks be to God.

(Short Form)

Brothers, I beg you through the mercy of God to offer your bodies as a living sacrifice holy and acceptable to God, your spiritual worship. Do not conform yourselves to this age but be transformed by the renewal of your mind so that you may judge what is God's will, what is good, pleasing and perfect.

Your love must be sincere. Detest what is evil, cling to what is good. Love one another with the affection of brothers. Anticipate each other in showing respect. Do not grow slack but be fervent in spirit; he whom you serve is the Lord. Rejoice in hope, be patient under trial, persevere in prayer. Look on the needs of the saints as your own; be generous in offering hospitality.

This is the Word of the Lord.

℟. Thanks be to God.

3 77. 1 Cor 6, 13-15. 17-20

A reading from the first letter of Paul to the Corinthians

Your body is a temple of the Spirit.

The body is not for immorality; it is for the Lord, and the Lord is for the body. God, who raised up the Lord, will raise us also by his power. Do you not see that your bodies are members of Christ? But whoever is joined to the Lord becomes one spirit with him. Shun lewd conduct. Every other sin a man commits is outside his body, but the fornicator sins against his own body. You must know that your body is a temple of the Holy Spirit, who is within—the Spirit you have received from God. You are not your own. You have been purchased, and at what a price! So glorify God in your body.

This is the Word of the Lord.

℟. Thanks be to God.

4 78. 1 Cor 12, 31—13, 8

A reading from the first letter of Paul to the Corinthians

If I am without love, it will do me no good whatever.

Set your hearts on the greater gifts. I will show you the way which surpasses all the others. If I speak with human tongues and angelic as well, but do not have love, I am a noisy gong, a clanging cymbal. If I have the gift of prophecy and, with full knowledge, comprehend all mysteries, if I have faith great enough to move mountains, but have not love, I am nothing. If I give everything I have to feed the poor and hand over my body to be burned, but have not love, I gain nothing.

Love is patient; love is kind. Love is not jealous, it does not put on airs, it is not snobbish. Love is never rude, it is not self-seeking, it is not prone to anger; neither does it brood over injuries. Love does not rejoice in what is wrong but rejoices with the truth. There is no limit to love's forbearance, to its trust, its hope, its power to endure.

Love never fails.

This is the Word of the Lord.

℟. Thanks be to God.

5

79. Eph 5, 2. 21-33 or 5, 2. 25-32

A reading from the letter of Paul to the Ephesians

This mystery has many implications, and I am saying it applies to Christ and the Church.

(Long Form)

Follow the way of love, even as Christ loved you. He gave himself for us.

Defer to one another out of reverence for Christ.

Wives should be submissive to their husbands as if to the Lord because the husband is head of his wife just as Christ is head of his body the church, as well as its savior. As the church submits to Christ, so wives sould submit to their husbands in everything.

Husbands, love your wives, as Christ loved the church. He gave himself up for her to make her holy, purifying her in the bath of water by the power of the word, to present to himself a glorious church, holy and immaculate, without stain or wrinkle or anything of that sort. Husbands should love their wives as they do their own bodies. He who loves his wife loves himself. Observe that no one ever hates his own flesh; no, he nourishes

it and takes care of it as Christ cares for the church—for we are members of his body.

"For this reason a man shall leave his father and mother,
and shall cling to his wife,
and the two shall be made into one."

This is a great foreshadowing; I mean that it refers to Christ and the church. In any case, each one should love his wife as he loves himself, the wife for her part showing respect for her husband.

This is the Word of the Lord.

℟. Thanks be to God.

(Short Form)

Follow the way of love, even as Christ loved you. He gave himself for us.

Husbands, love your wives, as Christ loved the church. He gave himself up for her to make her holy, purifying her in the bath of water by the power of the word, to present to himself a glorious church, holy and immaculate, without stain or wrinkle or anything of that sort. Husbands should love their wives as they do their own bodies. He who loves his wife loves himself. Observe that no one ever hates his own flesh; no, he nourishes it and takes care of it as Christ cares for the church—for we are members of his body.

"For this reason a man shall leave his father and mother,
and shall cling to his wife,
and the two shall be made into one."

This is a great foreshadowing; I mean that it refers to Christ and the church.

This is the Word of the Lord.

℟. Thanks be to God.

6

80. Col 3, 12-17

A reading from the letter of Paul to the Colossians

Above all have love, which is the bond of perfection.

Because you are God's chosen ones, holy and beloved, clothe yourselves with heartfelt mercy, with kindness, humility, meekness, and patience. Bear with one another; forgive whatever grievances you have against one another. Forgive as the Lord has forgiven you. Over all these virtues put on love, which binds the rest together and makes them perfect. Christ's peace must reign in your hearts, since as members of the one body you have been called to that peace. Dedicate yourselves to thankfulness. Let the word of Christ, rich as it is, dwell in you. In wisdom made perfect, instruct and admonish one another. Sing gratefully to God from your hearts in psalms, hymns, and inspired songs. Whatever you do, whether in speech or in action, do it in the name of the Lord Jesus. Give thanks to God the Father through him.

This is the Word of the Lord.

℟. Thanks be to God.

7

81. 1 Pt 3, 1-9

A reading from the first letter of Peter

You should agree with one another, be sympathetic and love the brothers.

You married women must obey your husbands, so that any of them who do not believe in the word of the gospel may be won over apart from preaching, through their wives' conduct. They have only to observe the reverent purity of your way of life. The affectation of an elaborate hairdress, the wearing of golden jewelry, or the donning of rich robes is not for you. Your adornment is rather the hidden character of the heart, expressed in the unfading beauty of a calm and gentle disposition. This is precious in God's eyes. The holy women of past ages used to adorn

themselves in this way, reliant on God and obedient to their husbands—for example, Sarah, who was subject to Abraham and called him her master. You are her children when you do what is right and let no fears alarm you.

You husbands, too, must show consideration for those who share your lives. Treat women with respect as the weaker sex, heirs just as much as you to the gracious gift of life. If you do so, nothing will keep your prayers from being answered.

In summary, then, all of you should be like-minded, sympathetic, loving toward one another, kindly disposed, and humble. Do not return evil for evil or insult for insult. Return a blessing instead. This you have been called to do, that you may receive a blessing as your inheritance.

This is the Word of the Lord.

℟. Thanks be to God.

8

82. 1 Jn 3, 18-24

A reading from the first letter of John

Our love is to be something real and active.

Little children,
let us love in deed and in truth,
and not merely talk about it.
This is our way of knowing we are committed to the truth
and are at peace before him
no matter what our consciences may charge us with;
for God is greater than our hearts
and all is known to him.
Beloved,
if our consciences have nothing to charge us with,
we can be sure that God is with us
and that we will receive at his hands
whatever we ask.

Why? Because we are keeping his commandments
and doing what is pleasing in his sight.
His commandment is this:
we are to believe in the name of his Son, Jesus Christ,
and are to love one another as he commanded us.
Those who keep his commandments remain in him
and he in them.
And this is how we know that he remains in us:
from the Spirit that he gave us.

This is the Word of the Lord.

℟. Thanks be to God.

9

83. 1 Jn 4, 7-12

A reading from the first letter of John

God is love.

Beloved,
let us love one another
because love is of God;
everyone who loves is begotten of God
and has knowledge of God.
The man without love has known nothing of God,
for God is love.
God's love was revealed in our midst in this way:
he sent his only Son to the world
that we might have life through him.
Love, then, consists in this:
not that we have loved God,
but that he has loved us
and has sent his Son as an offering for our sins.
Beloved,
if God has loved us so,
we must have the same love for one another.
No one has ever seen God.

Yet if we love one another
God dwells in us,
and his love is brought to perfection in us.

This is the Word of the Lord.

℟. Thanks be to God.

10 **84.** Rv 19, 1. 5-9

A reading from the book of Revelation

Happy are those who are invited to the wedding feast of the Lamb.

I, John, heard what sounded like the loud song of a great assembly in heaven. They were singing:

"Alleluia!
Salvation, glory, and might belong to our God."

A voice coming from the throne cried out: "Praise our God, all you his servants, the small and the great, who revere him!" Then I heard what sounded like the shouts of a great crowd, or the roaring of the deep, or mighty peals of thunder, as they cried:

"Alleluia!
The Lord is king,
our God, the Almighty!
Let us rejoice and be glad,
and give him glory!
For this is the wedding day of the Lamb,
his bride has prepared herself for the wedding.
She has been given a dress to wear
made of finest linen, brilliant white."

(The linen dress is the virtuous deeds of God's saints.)

The angel then said to me: "Write this down: Happy are they who have been invited to the wedding feast of the Lamb."

This is the Word of the Lord.

℟. Thanks be to God.

RESPONSORIAL PSALM

The cantor of the psalm sings or recites the psalm, and the people make the response.

1 **85.** Ps 33, 12. 18. 20-21. 22

℟. (5) The earth is full of the goodness of the Lord.

Happy the nation whose God is the Lord,
the people he has chosen for his own inheritance.
But see, the eyes of the Lord are upon those who fear him,
upon those who hope for his kindness.

℟ The earth is full of the goodness of the Lord.

Our soul waits for the Lord,
who is our help and our shield,
For in him our hearts rejoice;
in his holy name we trust.

℟. The earth is full of the goodness of the Lord.

May your kindness, O Lord, be upon us
who have put our hope in you.

℟. The earth is full of the goodness of the Lord.

2 **86.** Ps 34, 2-3. 4-5. 6-7. 8-9

℟. (2) I will bless the Lord at all times.

I will bless the Lord at all times;
his praise shall be ever in my mouth.
Let my soul glory in the Lord;
the lowly will hear me and be glad.

℟. I will bless the Lord at all times.

Glorify the Lord with me,
let us together extol his name.
I sought the Lord, and he answered me
and delivered me from all my fears.

℟. I will bless the Lord at all times.

Look to him that you may be radiant with joy,
and your faces may not blush with shame.
When the afflicted man called out, the Lord heard,
and from all his distress he saved him.

℟. I will bless the Lord at all times.

The angel of the Lord encamps
around those who fear him, and delivers them.
Taste and see how good the Lord is;
happy the man who takes refuge in him.

℟. I will bless the Lord at all times.

℟. Or: (9) Taste and see the goodness of the Lord.

3 **87.** Ps 103, 1-2. 8. 13. 17-18

℟. (8) The Lord is kind and merciful.

Bless the Lord, O my soul;
and all my being, bless his holy name.
Bless the Lord, O my soul,
and forget not all his benefits.

℟. The Lord is kind and merciful.

Merciful and gracious is the Lord,
slow to anger and abounding in kindness.
As a father has compassion on his children,
so the Lord has compassion on those who fear him.

℟. The Lord is kind and merciful.

But the kindness of the Lord is from eternity
to eternity toward those who fear him,
And his justice toward children's children
among those who keep his covenant.

℟. The Lord is kind and merciful.

℟. Or: (17) The Lord's kindness is everlasting
to those who fear him.

4

88. Ps 112, 1-2. 3-4. 5-7. 7-8. 9

℟. (1) Happy are those who do what the Lord commands.

Happy the man who fears the Lord,
who greatly delights in his commands.
His posterity shall be mighty upon the earth;
the upright generation shall be blessed.

℟. Happy are those who do what the Lord commands.

Wealth and riches shall be in his house;
his generosity shall endure forever.
He dawns through the darkness, a light for the upright;
he is gracious and merciful and just.

℟. Happy are those who do what the Lord commands.

Well for the man who is gracious and lends,
who conducts his affairs with justice;
He shall never be moved;
the just man shall be in everlasting remembrance.

℟. Happy are those who do what the Lord commands.

An evil report he shall not fear.
His heart is firm, trusting in the Lord.
His heart is steadfast; he shall not fear
till he looks down upon his foes.

℟. Happy are those who do what the Lord commands.

Lavishly he gives to the poor;
his generosity shall endure forever;
his horn shall be exalted in glory.

℟. Happy are those who do what the Lord commands.

℟. Or: Alleluia.

5

89. Ps 128, 1-2. 3. 4-5

℟. (1) Happy are those who fear the Lord.

Happy are you who fear the Lord,
who walk in his ways!
For you shall eat the fruit of your handiwork;
happy shall you be, and favored.

℟. Happy are those who fear the Lord.

Your wife shall be like a fruitful vine
in the recesses of your home;
Your children like olive plants
around your table.

℟. Happy are those who fear the Lord.

Behold, thus is the man blessed
who fears the Lord.
The Lord bless you from Zion:
may you see the prosperity of Jerusalem
all the days of your life.

℟. Happy are those who fear the Lord.

℟. Or: (4) See how the Lord blesses those who fear him.

6

90. Ps 145, 8-9. 10. 15. 17-18

℟. (9) The Lord is compassionate to all his creatures.

The Lord is gracious and merciful,
slow to anger and of great kindness.
The Lord is good to all
and compassionate toward all his works.

℟. The Lord is compassionate to all his creatures.

Let all your works give you thanks, O Lord,
and let your faithful ones bless you.
The eyes of all look hopefully to you,
and you give them their food in due season.

℟. The Lord is compassionate to all his creatures.

The Lord is just in all his ways
and holy in all his works.
The Lord is near to all who call upon him,
to all who call upon him in truth.

℟. The Lord is compassionate to all his creatures.

7 **91.** Ps 148, 1-2. 3-4. 9-10. 11-12. 12-14

℟. (12) Let all praise the name of the Lord.

Praise the Lord from the heavens,
praise him in the heights;
Praise him, all you his angels,
praise him, all you his hosts.

℟. Let all praise the name of the Lord.

Praise him, sun and moon;
praise him, all you shining stars.
Praise him, you highest heavens,
and you waters above the heavens.

℟. Let all praise the name of the Lord.

You mountains and all you hills,
you fruit trees and all you cedars;
You wild beasts and all tame animals,
you creeping things and you winged fowl.

℟. Let all praise the name of the Lord.

Let the kings of the earth and all peoples,
the princes and all the judges of the earth,
Young men too, and maidens,
old men and boys.

℟. Let all praise the name of the Lord.

Praise the name of the Lord,
for his name alone is exalted;
His majesty is above earth and heaven,
and he has lifted up the horn of his people.

℟. Let all praise the name of the Lord.

℟. Or: Alleluia.

ALLELUIA VERSE AND VERSE BEFORE THE GOSPEL

1 — 92. 1 Jn 4, 8. 11

God is love;
let us love one another as he has loved us.

2 — 93. 1 Jn 4, 12

If we love one another,
God will live in us in perfect love.

3 — 94. 1 Jn 4, 16

He who lives in love, lives in God,
and God in him.

4 — 95. 1 Jn 4-7b

Everyone who loves is born of God and knows him.

GOSPEL

1 96. Mt 5, 1-12

℣. **The Lord be with you.**

℟. And also with you.

✠ **A reading from the holy gospel according to Matthew**

℟. Glory to you, Lord.

Rejoice and be glad, for your reward will be great in heaven.

When Jesus saw the crowds he went up on the mountainside. After he had sat down his disciples gathered around him, and he began to teach them:

"How blest are the poor in spirit: the reign of God is theirs.
Blest too are the sorrowing; they shall be consoled.
[Blest are the lowly; they shall inherit the land.]
Blest are they who hunger and thirst for holiness;
they shall have their fill.
Blest are they who show mercy; mercy shall be theirs.
Blest are the single-hearted for they shall see God.
Blest too the peacemakers; they shall be called sons of God.
Blest are those persecuted for holiness' sake; the reign of God is theirs.
Blest are you when they insult you and persecute you and utter every kind of slander against you because of me.
Be glad and rejoice, for your reward in heaven is great."

This is the gospel of the Lord.

℟. Praise to you, Lord Jesus Christ.

2

97. Mt 5, 13-16

℣. **The Lord be with you.** ℟. And also with you.

✠ **A reading from the holy gospel according to Matthew**

℟. Glory to you, Lord.

You are the light of the world.

Jesus said to his disciples: "You are the salt of the earth. But what if salt goes flat? How can you restore its flavor? Then it is good for nothing but to be thrown out and trampled underfoot.

"You are the light of the world. A city set on a hill cannot be hidden. Men do not light a lamp and then put it under a bushel basket. They set it on a stand where it gives light to all in the house. In the same way, your light must shine before men so that they may see goodness in your acts and give praise to your heavenly Father."

This is the gospel of the Lord.

℟. Praise to you, Lord Jesus Christ.

3

98. Mt 7, 21. 24-29 or 7, 21. 24-25

℣. **The Lord be with you.** ℟. And also with you.

✠ **A reading from the holy gospel according to Matthew**

℟. Glory to you, Lord.

He built his house on rock.

(Long Form)

Jesus said to his disciples: "None of those who cry out, 'Lord, Lord,' will enter the kingdom of God but only the one who does the will of my Father in heaven.

"Anyone who hears my words and puts them into practice is like the wise man who built his house on rock. When the rainy season set in, the torrents came and the winds blew and buffeted

his house. It did not collapse; it had been solidly set on rock. Anyone who hears my words but does not put them into practice is like the foolish man who built his house on sandy ground. The rains fell, the torrents came, the winds blew and lashed against his house. It collapsed under all this and was completely ruined."

Jesus finished this discourse and left the crowds spellbound at his teaching. The reason was that he taught with authority and not like the scribes.

OR

(Short Form)

Jesus said to his disciples: "None of those who cry out, 'Lord, Lord,' will enter the kingdom of God but only the one who does the will of my Father in heaven.

"Anyone who hears my words and puts them into practice is like the wise man who built his house on rock. When the rainy season set in, the torrents came and the winds blew and buffeted his house. It did not collapse; it had been solidly set on rock."

This is the gospel of the Lord.

℟. Praise to you, Lord Jesus Christ.

4

99. Mt 19, 3-6

℣. **The Lord be with you.** ℟. And also with you.

✠ **A reading from the holy gospel according to Matthew**

℟. Glory to you, Lord.

So then, what God has united, man must not divide.

Some Pharisees came up to Jesus and said, to test him, "May a man divorce his wife for any reason whatever?" He replied, "Have you not read that at the beginning the Creator made them male and female and declared, 'For this reason a man shall leave his father and mother and cling to his wife, and the two shall

become as one'? Thus they are no longer two but one flesh. Therefore, let no man separate what God has joined."

This is the gospel of the Lord.

℟. Praise to you, Lord Jesus Christ.

5

100. Mt 22, 35-40

℣. **The Lord be with you.** ℟. And also with you.

✠ **A reading from the holy gospel according to Matthew**

℟. Glory to you, Lord.

This is the greatest and the first commandment. The second is similar to it.

One of the Pharisees, a lawyer, in an attempt to trip up Jesus, asked him, "Teacher, which commandment of the law is the greatest?" Jesus said to him:

" 'You shall love the Lord your God
with your whole heart,
with your whole soul,
and with all your mind.'

This is the greatest and first commandment. The second is like it:

'You shall love your neighbor as yourself.'

On these two commandments the whole law is based, and the prophets as well."

This is the gospel of the Lord.

℟. Praise to you, Lord Jesus Christ.

6

101. Mk 10, 6-9

℣. **The Lord be with you.** ℟. And also with you.

✠ **A reading from the holy gospel according to Mark**

℟. Glory to you, Lord.

They are no longer two, therefore, but one body.

Jesus said: "At the beginning of creation God made them male and female; for this reason a man shall leave his father and

mother and the two shall become as one. They are no longer two but one flesh. Therefore let no man separate what God has joined."

This is the gospel of the Lord.

℟. Praise to you, Lord Jesus Christ.

7

102. Jn 2, 1-11

℣. **The Lord be with you.** ℟. And also with you.

✠ **A reading from the holy gospel according to John**

℟. Glory to you, Lord.

This was the first of the signs given by Jesus; it was given at Cana in Galilee.

There was a wedding at Cana in Galilee, and the mother of Jesus was there. Jesus and his disciples had likewise been invited to the celebration. At a certain point the wine ran out, and Jesus' mother told him, "They have no more wine." Jesus replied, "Woman, how does this concern of yours involve me? My hour has not yet come." His mother instructed those waiting on table, "Do whatever he tells you." As prescribed for Jewish ceremonial washings, there were at hand six stone water jars, each one holding fifteen to twenty-five gallons. "Fill those jars with water," Jesus ordered, at which they filled them to the brim. "Now," he said, "draw some out and take it to the waiter in charge." They did as he instructed them. The waiter in charge tasted the water made wine, without knowing where it had come from; only the waiters knew since they had drawn the water. Then the waiter in charge called the groom over and remarked to him: "People usually serve the choice wine first; then when the guests have been drinking a while, a lesser vintage. What you have

done is keep the choice wine until now." Jesus performed this first of his signs at Cana in Galilee. Thus did he reveal his glory, and his disciples believed in him.

This is the gospel of the Lord.

℟. Praise to you, Lord Jesus Christ.

8 103. Jn 15, 9-12

℣. **The Lord be with you.** ℟. And also with you.

✠ **A reading from the holy gospel according to John**

℟. Glory to you, Lord.

Remain in my love.

Jesus said to his disciples:
"As the Father has loved me,
so I have loved you.
Live on in my love.
You will live in my love
if you keep my commandments,
even as I have kept my Father's commandments,
and live in his love.
All this I tell you
that my joy may be yours
and your joy may be complete.
This is my commandment:
love one another
as I have loved you."

This is the gospel of the Lord.

℟. Praise to you, Lord Jesus Christ.

9

104. Jn 15, 12-16

℣. **The Lord be with you.** ℟. And also with you.

✠ **A reading from the holy gospel according to John**

℟. Glory to you, Lord.

This is my commandment: love one another.

Jesus said to his disciples:
"This is my commandment:
love one another
as I have loved you.
There is no greater love than this:
to lay down one's life for one's friends.
You are my friends
if you do what I command you.
I no longer speak of you as slaves,
for a slave does not know what his master is about.
Instead, I call you friends,
since I have made known to you all that I heard from my Father.
It was not you who chose me,
it was I who chose you
to go forth and bear fruit.
Your fruit must endure,
so that all you ask the Father in my name
he will give you."

This is the gospel of the Lord.

℟. Praise to you, Lord Jesus Christ.

10 105. Jn 17, 20-26 or 17, 20-23

℣. **The Lord be with you.** ℟. And also with you.

✠ **A reading from the holy gospel according to John**

℟. Glory to you, Lord.

May they be completely one.

(Long Form)

Jesus looked up to heaven and prayed:

"Holy Father,
I do not pray for my disciples alone.
I pray also for those who will believe in me through their word,
that all may be one
as you, Father, are in me, and I in you;
I pray that they may be [one] in us,
that the world may believe that you sent me.
I have given them the glory you gave me
that they may be one, as we are one—
I living in them, you living in me—
that their unity may be complete.
So shall the world know that you sent me,
and that you loved them as you loved me.
Father,
all those you gave me
I would have in my company
where I am,
to see this glory of mine
which is your gift to me,
because of the love you bore me before the world began.
Just Father,
the world has not known you,
but I have known you;
and these men have known that you sent me.

To them I have revealed your name,
and I will continue to reveal it
so that your love for me may live in them,
and I may live in them."

OR
(Short Form)

Jesus looked up to heaven and prayed:
"Holy Father,
I do not pray for my disciples alone.
I pray also for those who will believe in me through their word,
that all may be one
as you, Father, are in me, and I in you;
I pray that they may be [one] in us,
that the world may believe that you sent me.
I have given them the glory you gave me
that they may be one, as we are one—
I living in them, you living in me—
that their unity may be complete.
So shall the world know that you sent me,
and that you loved them as you loved me."
This is the gospel of the Lord.

℟. Praise to you, Lord Jesus Christ.

II. OPENING PRAYERS

1 106.

**Father,
you have made the bond of marriage
a holy mystery,
a symbol of Christ's love for his Church.
Hear our prayers for N. and N.
With faith in you and in each other
they pledge their love today.
May their lives always bear witness
to the reality of that love.**

**We ask you this
through our Lord Jesus Christ, your Son,
who lives and reigns with you and the Holy Spirit,
one God, for ever and ever.**

2 107.

**Father,
hear our prayers for N. and N.,
who today are united in marriage before your altar.
Give them your blessing,
and strengthen their love for each other.**

**We ask you this
through our Lord . . .**

3

Almighty God, 108.
hear our prayers for N. and N.,
who have come here today
to be united in the sacrament of marriage.
Increase their faith in you and in each other,
and through them bless your Church
(with Christian children).

We ask you this
through our Lord . . .

4 109.

Father,
when you created mankind
you willed that man and wife should be one.
Bind N. and N.
in the loving union of marriage;
and make their love fruitful
so that they may be living witnesses
to your divine love in the world.

We ask you this
through our Lord . . .

III. BLESSING OF RINGS

1 110.

Lord, bless these rings which we bless ✠ in your name.
Grant that those who wear them
may always have a deep faith in each other.
May they do your will
and always live together
in peace, good will, and love.
We ask this through Christ our Lord.
℟. Amen.

2 111.

Lord,
bless ✠ and consecrate N. and N.
in their love for each other.
May these rings be a symbol
of true faith in each other,
and always remind them of their love.
We ask this through Christ our Lord.
℟. Amen.

IV. PRAYERS OVER THE GIFTS

1

Lord, **112.**
accept our offering
for this newly-married couple, N. and N.
By your love and providence you have brought
them together;
now bless them all the days of their married life.
We ask this through Christ our Lord.

2

Lord, **113.**
accept the gifts we offer you
on this happy day.
In your fatherly love
watch over and protect N. and N.
whom you have united in marriage.
We ask this through Christ our Lord.

3

Lord, **114.**
hear our prayers
and accept the gifts we offer for N. and N.
Today you have made them one in the sacrament of marriage.
May the mystery of Christ's unselfish love,
which we celebrate in this eucharist,
increase their love for you and for each other.
We ask this through Christ our Lord.

V. PREFACES

1 115.

**Father, all-powerful and ever-living God,
we do well always and everywhere to give you thanks.
By this sacrament your grace unites man and woman
in an unbreakable bond of love and peace.**

**You have designed the chaste love of husband and wife
for the increase both of the human family
and of your own family born in baptism.
You are the loving Father of the world of nature;
you are the loving Father of the new creation of grace.
In Christian marriage you bring together the two orders of creation:
nature's gift of children enriches the world
and your grace enriches also your Church.**

**Through Christ the choirs of angels
and all the saints
praise and worship your glory.
May our voices blend with theirs
as we join in their unending hymn:**

2 116.

**Father, all powerful and ever-living God,
we do well always and everywhere to give you thanks
through Jesus Christ our Lord.**

**Through him you entered into a covenant with your people.
You restored man to grace in the saving mystery of redemption.
You gave him a share in the divine life**

through his union with Christ.
You made him an heir of Christ's eternal glory.

This outpouring of love in the new covenant of grace
is symbolized in the marriage covenant
that seals the love of husband and wife
and reflects your divine plan of love.

And so, with the angels and all the saints in heaven
we proclaim your glory
and join in their unending hymn of praise:

3

Father, all powerful and ever-living God, 117.
we do well always and everywhere to give you thanks.

You created man in love to share your divine life.
We see his high destiny in the love of husband and wife,
which bears the imprint of your own divine love.

Love is man's origin,
love is his constant calling,
love is his fulfillment in heaven.

The love of man and woman
is made holy in the sacrament of marrige
and becomes the mirror of your everlasting love.

Through Christ the choirs of angels
and all the saints
praise and worship your glory.
May our voices blend with theirs
as we join in their unending hymn:

VI. HANC IGITUR

118. The words in parentheses may be omitted if desired.

Father, accept this offering
from your whole family
and from N. and N. for whom we now pray.
You have brought them to their wedding day:
grant them (the gift and joy of children and)
a long and happy life together.
(Through Christ our Lord. Amen.)

VII. NUPTIAL BLESSING

1

119. *Father, by your power,* with the proper invitatory, as in no. 33.

2

120. In the following prayer, either the paragraph *Holy Father, you created mankind,* or the paragraph *Father, to reveal the plan of your love,* may be omitted, keeping only the paragraph which corresponds to the reading of the Mass.

The priest faces the bride and bridegroom and, with hands joined, says:

Let us pray to the Lord for N. and N.
who come to God's altar at the beginning of their married life
so that they may always be united in love for each other
(as now they share in the body and blood of Christ).

All pray silently for a short while. Then the priest extends his hands and continues:

Holy Father, you created mankind in your own image
and made man and woman to be joined as husband and wife
in union of body and heart
and so fulfill their mission in this world.

Father, to reveal the plan of your love,
you made the union of husband and wife
an image of the covenant between you and your people.
In the fulfillment of this sacrament,
the marriage of Christian man and woman
is a sign of the marriage between Christ and the Church.
Father, stretch out your hand, and bless N. and N.

Lord, grant that as they begin to live this sacrament
they may share with each other the gifts of your love

and become one in heart and mind
as witnesses to your presence in their marriage.
Help them to create a home together
(and give them children to be formed by the gospel
and to have a place in your family).

Give your blessing to N., your daughter,
so that she may be a good wife (and mother),
caring for the home,
faithful in love for her husband,
generous and kind.
Give your blessings to N., your son,
so that he may be a faithful husband
(and a good father).

Father, grant as they come together to your table on earth,
so they may one day have the joy of sharing your feast in heaven.

We ask this through Christ our Lord.

℟. **Amen.**

3

The priest faces the bride and bridegroom and, with hands joined, says:

121.

My dear friends, let us ask God
for his continued blessings upon this bridegroom and his bride (or N. and N).

All pray silently for a short while. Then the priest extends his hands and continues:

Holy Father, creator of the universe,
maker of man and woman in your own likeness,
source of blessing for married life,

source of blessing for married life,
we humbly pray to you for this woman
who today is united with her husband in this sacrament of marriage.

May your fullest blessing come upon her and her husband
so that they may together rejoice in your gift of married love
(and enrich your Church with their children).

Lord, may they both praise you when they are happy
and turn to you in their sorrows.
May they be glad that you help them in their work
and know that you are with them in their need.
May they pray to you in the community of the Church,
and be your witnesses in the world.
May they reach old age in the company of their friends,
and come at last to the kingdom of heaven.
(We ask this) through Christ our Lord.
℟. **Amen.**

VIII. PRAYERS AFTER COMMUNION

1

Lord, 122.
in your love
you have given us this eucharist
to unite us with one another and with you.
As you have made N. **and** N.
one in this sacrament of marriage
(**and in the sharing of the one bread and the one cup**),
so now make them one in love for each other.

We ask this through Christ our Lord.
℟. Amen.

2 123.

Lord,
we who have shared the food of your table
pray for our friends N. **and** N.,
whom you have joined together in marriage.
Keep them close to you always.
May their love for each other
proclaim to all the world
their faith in you.

We ask this through Christ our Lord.
℟. Amen.

3 124.

Almighty God,
may the sacrifice we have offered
and the eucharist we have shared
strengthen the love of N. **and** N.,
and give us all your fatherly aid.

We ask this through Christ our Lord.
℟. Amen.

IX. BLESSING AT THE END OF MASS

1 125.

God the eternal Father keep you in love with each other,
so that the peace of Christ may stay with you
and be always in your home.
℟. **Amen.**
May (your children bless you)
your friends console you
and all men live in peace with you.
℟. **Amen.**

May you always bear witness to the love of God in this world
so that the afflicted and the needy
will find in you generous friends,
and welcome you into the joys of heaven.
℟. **Amen.**

And may almighty God bless you all,
the Father, and the Son, ✠ and the Holy Spirit.
℟. **Amen.**

2 126.

May God, the almighty Father,
give you his joy
and bless you (in your children).
℟. **Amen.**

May the only Son of God have mercy on you
and help you in good times and in bad.

℟. **Amen.**

May the Holy Spirit of God
always fill your hearts with his love.

℟. **Amen.**

And may almighty God bless you all,
the Father, and the Son, ✠ and the Holy Spirit.

℟. **Amen.**

3

127.

May the Lord Jesus, who was a guest at the wedding in Cana,
bless you and your families and friends.

℟. **Amen.**

May Jesus, who loved his Church to the end,
always fill your hearts with his love.

℟. **Amen.**

May he grant that, as you believe in his resurrection,
so you may wait for him in joy and hope.

℟. **Amen.**

And may almighty God bless you all,
the Father, and the Son, ✠ and the Holy Spirit.

℟. **Amen.**

4

In the United States

May almighty God, with his Word of blessing, unite your hearts in the never-ending bond of pure love.

℟. Amen.

May your children bring you happiness, and may your generous love for them be returned to you, many times over.

℟. Amen.

May the peace of Christ live always in your hearts and in your home.
May you have true friends to stand by you, both in joy and in sorrow.
May you be ready and willing to help and comfort all who come to you in need.
And may the blessings promised to the compassionate be yours in abundance.

℟. Amen.

May you find happiness and satisfaction in your work. May daily problems never cause you undue anxiety, nor the desire for earthly possessions dominate your lives. But may your heart's first desire be always the good things waiting for you in the life of heaven.

℟. Amen.

May the Lord bless you with many happy years together, so that you may enjoy the rewards of a good life. And after you have served him loyally in his kingdom on earth, may he welcome you to his eternal kingdom in heaven.

℟. Amen.

And may almighty God bless you all,
the Father, and the Son, ✠ and the Holy Spirit.

℟. Amen.

APPENDIX I

(From the General Instruction to the Roman Missal, nos. 240-152)

Communion under Both Kinds

240. The sign of communion is more complete when given under both kinds, since the sign of the eucharistic meal appears more clearly. The intention of Christ that the new and eternal covenant be ratified in his blood is better expressed, as is the relation of the eucharistic banquet to the heavenly banquet.

241. Priests should use the occasion to teach the faithful the Catholic doctrine on the form of communion, as affirmed by the Council of Trent. They should first be reminded that, according to Catholic faith, they receive the whole Christ and the genuine sacrament when they participate in the sacrament even under one kind and that they are not thus deprived of any grace necessary for salvation.

They should also be taught that, provided the matter and form are safeguarded, the Church may change the manner of celebrating and receiving the sacraments. In doing so it judges when such changes will better meet the devotion or needs of different times and places. At the same time they should be urged to take part in the rite which brings out the sign of the eucharistic meal more fully.

242. With the bishop's approval and after the necessary explanation, communion from the chalice is permitted for . . . (2) the bride and bridegroom at their wedding Mass . . . [and] (11) those . . . celebrating their [wedding] jubilees.

243. Preparations for giving communion under both kinds:

(a) If communion is received from the chalice with a tube, silver tubes are needed for the celebrant and each communicant. There should also be a container of water to wash the tubes and a paten on which to place them.

(b) If communion is given with a spoon, only one spoon is necessary.

(c) If communion is given by intinction, the host should not be too thin or too small, but a little thicker than usual so that it may be partly dipped in the blood and easily given to the communicant.

(1) Communion under Both Kinds from the Chalice

244. If there is a deacon or another priest:

(a) The celebrant receives communion as usual, making sure enough remains in the chalice for the other communicants. He wipes the outside of the chalice with a purificator.

(b) Giving the chalice and purificator to the deacon, the celebrant takes the paten or other vessel with the hosts, and both go to the convenient place for the communion of the faithful.

(c) The communicants approach, make a suitable reverence, and stand in front of the celebrant. He holds the host slightly raised and says: The body of Christ. The communicant answers: Amen, and receives it.

(d) The communicant then stands before the deacon, who says: The blood of Christ. The communicant answers: Amen, and the deacon holds out the chalice and purificator. The communicant raises the chalice to his mouth with his own hands, taking care not to spill it. He holds the purificator under his mouth with his left hand, drinks a little from the chalice, and then returns to his place. The deacon wipes the outside of the chalice with the purificator.

(e) The deacon places the chalice on the altar after all who are receiving under both kinds have drunk from it. If there are others who do not receive communion under both kinds, the celebrant returns to the altar when he finishes giving communion to them. The celebrant or deacon drinks whatever remains in the chalice, and it is cleansed in the usual way.

245. If there is no deacon or other priest:

(a) The celebrant receives communion as usual, making sure enough remains in the chalice for the other communicants. He wipes the outside of the chalice with the purificator.

(b) The celebrant then goes to a convenient place and distributes the body of Christ as usual to all who are receiving under both kinds. The communicants approach, make a suitable reverence, and stand in front of the celebrant. After receiving the body of Christ, they step back a little.

(c) After all have received, the celebrant places the vessel on the altar and takes the chalice and purificator. The communicants again come forward and stand in front of the celebrant. He says: The blood of Christ, the communicant answers: Amen, and the celebrant holds out the chalice and purificator. The communicant holds the purificator under his chin with his left hand, taking care that none of the precious blood is spilled, drinks a little from the chalice, and then returns to his place. The celebrant wipes the outside of the chalice with the purificator.

(d) The celebrant places the chalice on the altar after all who are receiving under both kinds have drunk from it. If others receive communion under one kind only, he gives it to them and then returns to the altar, where he consumes the remainder of the blood and cleanses the chalice in the usual way.

(2) Communion under Both Kinds by Intinction

246. If there is a deacon or another priest:

(a) The celebrant hands the deacon the chalice and purificator and takes the paten or other vessel with the hosts. Both go to a convenient place for distributing communion.

(b) The communicants approach, make a suitable reverence, and stand in front of the celebrant. Each holds the paten under his chin while the celebrant dips a particle into the chalice and, raising it, says: The body and blood of Christ. The communicant responds: Amen, receives it from the celebrant, and returns to his place.

(c) The communion of those who do not receive under both kinds and the rest of the rite take place as described above.

247. If there is no deacon or other priest:

(a) After drinking the blood of the Lord, the celebrant takes the paten with the hosts between the index and middle fingers of his left hand and holds the chalice between the thumb and index finger of the same hand. Then he goes to a convenient place for distributing communion.

(b) The communicants approach, make a suitable reverence, and stand in front of the celebrant. Each holds the paten under his chin while the celebrant takes a particle, dips it into the chalice, and holds it up, saying: The body and blood of Christ. The communicant responds: Amen, receives it from the celebrant, and returns to his place.

(c) It is also permitted to place a small table covered with a cloth and corporal on the first altar step or at the sanctuary entrance. The celebrant places the chalice on this table in order to make the distribution of communion easier.

(d) The communion of those who do not receive under both kinds and the rest of the rite take place as described above.

(3) Communion under Both Kinds from a Tube

248. The celebrant also uses a tube when receiving the blood of the Lord in this case.

249. If there is a deacon or another priest:

(a) For the communion of the body of the Lord, everything is done as described above, nos. 244b and 244c.

(b) The communicant goes to the deacon and stands in front of him. The deacon says: The blood of Christ, and the communicant responds: Amen. He receives the tube from the minister, places it in the chalice, and drinks a little. He then removes the tube, not spilling any drops, and places it in a container of water which is held by the minister next to the deacon. Then, to cleanse the tube, he drinks a little water from it and places it in a container held by the minister.

250. If there is no deacon or other priest, the celebrant offers the chalice to each communicant in the usual way (see no. 245). The ninister holds the container of water for cleansing the tube.

(4) Communion under Both Kinds from a Spoon

251. If a deacon or another priest assists, he holds the chalice in his left hand. Each communicant holds the paten under his chin while the deacon or priest gives him the blood of the Lord with the spoon, saying: The blood of Christ. The communicant should be careful not to touch the spoon with his lips or tongue.

252. If there is no deacon or other priest, the celebrant first gives the hosts to all who are receiving under both kinds and then gives them the blood of the Lord.

APPENDIX II

HOMILETIC NOTES FOR THE NEW READINGS

CLASSIFICATION OF THE READINGS ACCORDING TO SUBJECT

	First Readings (O.T.)	Second Readings (N.T.)	Gospels
Institution of Marriage	1. 2		4. 6
Accounts of Weddings	3. 4		
Sanctity of Marriage	5. 8	3. 5	7
Indissolubility of Marriage	2	(1.) 5	(3.) 4. 6
Peace and Prosperity of Homes	7	6. 7	2. 10
Primacy of Love	6	1. 4. 8 9	5. 8. 9 10
Christian Life		2	1. 3

FIRST READING

1 CREATION OF MAN AND WOMAN

(Gn 1, 26-28. 31)

Sacred Scripture has preserved for us the creation of the first couple in two accounts: Gn 1, 26-38. 31; Gn 2, 18-24. Both texts have been included in the readings of the new marriage rite.

Written from different theological viewpoints, each one emphasizes diverse particular aspects and so enriches the subject.

The priestly author of Gn 1, 26-28. 31, in accord with his purpose, places more stress on the aspect of conjugal society (man and woman are created at the same time) and on the couple's function with respect to fecundity and dominion of the earth.

The human couple is created in God's image (v 27), which places them on a plane superior to all other creatures, signified by their participation in the divine sovereignty over things (vv 28-30).

"God looked at everything he had made, and he found it very good" (v 31). The sacred author thus indicates that sexuality forms part of the total religious conception of man. Marriage is pleasing to God when it confirms a generous and freely given love.

PASTORAL NOTE — **This text does not require a high degree of biblical knowledge on the part of the people. However, it will be more readily understood by those with a solid religious background.**

---

2 UNITY AND INDISSOLUBILITY OF MARRIAGE

(Gn 2, 18-24)

Continuous solitude is not good (Eccl 4, 7-13). To remedy the solitude of man God creates woman, who is described in v 18 as "a suitable partner for him." This shows that woman is not a mere appendage of man ordered to his service but a complement possessing the same nature.

The creation of animals which the author intercalates in vv 19-20 has as its purpose to accentuate, by way of contrast, the true nature and role of woman: the animals who are "baptized" by man as a sign of his dominion over them (Gn 1, 26b. 28b) cannot be equated with man, for they are of an inferior nature (polemic against bestiality?).

Man is cast into a deep sleep, since he is not allowed to see God, especially during the process of creation. The image of the rib (of uncertain meaning; it might be related to the Sumerian word signifying both "rib" and "life"), the exclamation "bone of my bones and flesh of my flesh" (Gn 29, 14) as well as the stress on "woman" and "man" (vv 21-23)—all tend to underscore the profound unity and sexual attraction which exists between man and woman.

In clear and direct language verse 24 then proclaims the monogamous character of marriage in the initial order of things.

PASTORAL NOTE — **It is important for us to leave aside the details of the images presented and seek to uncover the profound significance of this text.**

Since Gospels no. 4 and 6 (Mt 16, 3-6 and Mk 10, 6-9) quote this text of Genesis verbatim, it would be well to choose one of them for the celebration in which this reading is used.

---

3 THE MARRIAGE OF ISAAC AND REBEKAH

(Gn 24, 48-51. 58-67)

In the course of the history of the People of God, marriage gradually loses in practice the lofty character which it possessed in the Genesis accounts. Despite this fact and despite the imperfections of the social order (excessive paternal authority and a certain absence of the freedom of choice), there are marriages in the history of Israel which correspond to the image of marriage in Genesis. The case of Isaac and Rebekah is one of them.

Even though marriage is above all a matter of civil right and the ancient texts make no reference to a religious ritual, the Israelite knows full well that God guides him in the choice of his wife (Gn 24, 42).

The power of conjugal love is praised. This love consoles Isaac in his sorrow over his mother's death. It is the fulfillment on the emotional plane of the truth that "a man leaves his father and mother and clings to his wife, and the two of them become one body."

PASTORAL NOTE — **This is a very simple text but it deals with a social climate very different from our own and thus must be correctly understood.**

---

4 MARRIAGE OF TOBIAH AND SARAH

(Tb 7, 9-10. 11-15)

The Book of Tobit, after the exile, gives a highly spiritual view of marriage and the home, prepared by God (Tb 3, 16), and founded on faith and prayer under his loving gaze (7, 11; 8, 4-9), in accord with the model traced by Genesis (8, 6; 2, 18).

In this reflection of the biblical ideal of marriage, the redeeming value of true love is also revealed: Sarah regains her health when she marries Tobiah, ending the curse cast upon her.

Like other biblical married couples: Isaac and Rebekah (Gn 24, 66), Jacob and Rachel (Gn 29, 20. 30), Boaz and Ruth (Ru 4, 13-15), Tobiah and Sarah bear witness to the presence of true love in the world.

In the general context of Tobiah's history, the account of his marriage is also a lesson of trust in Providence.

> PASTORAL NOTE — **This is a simple narrative that can be easily understood by all type of congregations. Mention should be made of the differences of the epoch in which it took place with respect to our own but it is not necessary to stress too much that we are dealing with an Old Testament text. We should also recall that the Entrance Song of the present Nuptial Mass as well as the final blessing are taken verbatim from this text.**

---

5 PRAYER OF TWO YOUNG SPOUSES

(Tb 8, 5-7)

This text is almost totally made up of a beautiful prayer addressed to God by Tobiah and Sarah on their wedding night. They ask God's blessing, but at the same time their prayer is a blessing of the Creator of human love.

Their blessing is motivated by the creation of all things, but it immediately becomes an evocation of the creation of the first couple: Adam and Eve, exalting the fundamental ideas in Genesis: fecundity, conjugal harmony, man-woman complement, fundamental equality.

The prayer is a manifestation of a love that is human and profoundly religious, capable of overcoming all selfish and profane motivation.

PASTORAL NOTE — **This second passage from Tobit is also quite simple and can appeal to sophisticated congregations.**

---

6 LOVE IS STERN AS DEATH

(Sg 2, 8-10. 14. 16. 8, 6-7)

The literal meaning of the Song of Songs is apparently allegorical in its entirety. The author describes the nuptial alliance of God and his People in human terms, but there is a messianic stamp from which it will receive its perfect fulfillment.

The bride, nostalgic because of her lover's absence, perceives his arrival. He comes speedily, anxious to see the one he loves with all his heart. She employs the image of the gazelle to describe the speed and grace of his approach.

The lover calls to her with a beautiful song of love. The season of spring, the flowers, the song of the dove, the vines in bloom—all constitute so many more reasons for consummating their espousals. Comparing her to the dove, he asks her to come out so that he can show her and give her all his love.

The lover concludes his song with the reassurance that love is stern as death.

This poem is included in the Bible precisely because human love is as it were the image and sacrament of the love that binds God and men.

PASTORAL NOTE — **This beautiful poem cannot be read to any congregation in general. It might be better simply to study it while the preparations for marriage are going on rather than to proclaim it in the liturgical action.**

---

7 THE WIFE, RADIANCE OF HER HOME

(Sir 26, 1-4. 13-16)

This is a sapiential poem, intended to sing the praises of a good wife. Basically, a good wife is a delight and a blessing to her husband: "Happy the husband of a good wife."

Such a wife is a blessing to her husband:

"Twice-lengthened are his days": a fundamental blessing, frequently found in the Deuteronomical preaching (Dt 5, 16-33; 6, 2; 11, 9).

"Peaceful and full is his life": another fundamental blessing. Such a gift surpasses all wealth, since it is a foundation of joy.

The praise of the goodness and beauty of a wife reaches its climax when she is compared to the sun rising in the Lord's heavens. The importance of this praise will be better understood by recalling what the author says about sunlight in the last chapters of the book.

PASTORAL NOTE — **This text can be used to counterbalance the vision of the wife completely subordinated to her husband which is imparted for example by the prayer for the wife in the nuptial blessing. When this reading is chosen, Gospel no. 2 (Mt 5, 13-16) could be used, since it invites all Christians—both men and women—to be the light of those who enter their home.**

8 THE NEW COVENANT OF THE PEOPLE OF GOD

(Jer 31, 31-32. 33-34)

From the summit of his prophetic tower, Jeremiah contemplates the past and the future. The essence and destiny of the People of God are always measured by the canon of the Covenant (Ez 16). At Sinai this People is born as a special possession of God, holy and consecrated (Ex 19, 5).

In the past, the Covenant is seen as a failure because of the infidelity of the people, in spite of their constant renovation (even recently, by the reform of Josiah: 2 Kgs 22—23). Thus, the inspired view of the prophet looks toward the future: God who is faithful will fulfill his plan, with a new and different Covenant, a work of his power and grace.

The aim of this New Covenant is identical to that of the Old: communion with him (v 33; 3, 29-40); the method is different: it is not an external juridical bond, but an interior realization sealed in the heart; with the grace of the effusion of his Spirit (Ez 36, 27; 37, 14; 39, 29; Jl 2, 28). God will imprint his will on man's heart.

The result will be a full and universal knowledge of God, that is, recognition, inner conversion, submission and offering, for an intimate and personal coexistence with God (Hos 2, 21-22; 4, 2; 6, 6, etc.).

PASTORAL NOTE — **This text does not refer directly to marriage Nevertheless, there is nothing artificial about its use for marriage. In the first place, every Christian home is a cell of the People of God and participates in the Covenant. Secondly, the very word Covenant evokes the marital union. How many times Sacred Scripture, from the prophets to the Book of Revelation, compares God's love for his people with married love! For the latter is a sign and sacrament of the former.**

If this text of Jeremiah is chosen, it would be well to choose as the Gospel one of the texts found in nos. 8, 9, 10 (Jn 15, 9-12, Jn 15, 12-16, or Jn 17, 20-26), which concern the eucharistic discourse and the priestly prayer of Christ, since they describe the fulfillment of the New Covenant prophesied by Jeremiah.

SECOND READING

1 WHO WILL SEPARATE US FROM THE LOVE OF CHRIST?

(Rom 8, 31-35. 37-39)

This text sounds like a triumphal hymn for the security of Christian hope.

The basis for firm hope lies in the fact that Christ, having given us the supreme gifts mentioned in v 34, can in no way stop loving us. Verse 35 enumerates the things that could make us doubt as to whether Christ still loves us: tribulations, distress, etc. Instead of depriving us of Christ's love, all these trials redound to our benefit; by the aid of Christ's love for us we overcome them all (v 37).

In verses 38-39 Paul lists the most powerful forces that might separate us from Christ and then reaches the inspiring affirmation that no created reality can cause such separation, which would entail the loss of all our graces based on the love of God and Christ.

PASTORAL NOTE — **This text does not speak directly of marriage but of Christ's love which forms the basis for its solidarity.**

Its meaning can be explained by the Gospels which speak about the indissolubility of marriage: nos. 4 and 6 (Mt 19, 3-6; Mk 10, 6-9). This reading can provide a better understanding of indissolubility, showing that it is not a negative attribute stemming solely from a positive will of God or the Church, but an essential characteristic of Christian love.

2 THE CHRISTIAN'S NEW LIFE

(Rm 12, 1-2. 9-18)

It would be most simplistic to regard chapter 12 of the Epistle to the Romans as a mere list of moral counsels.

There is a fundamental principle from which the entire moral life of the Christian springs: the whole of Christian life is a cultual sacrifice to God (v 1). The Christian's sacrifice consists not in offering or immolating things and animals but in offering himself by means of a good life.

The moral life of the Christian is the fruit of his conversion, that is, a radical change in mentality.

This provides the point of departure for the many exhortations which follow in the Epistle, from which those that refer to fraternal love have been selected here. And only in this light can the demands of Christian morality—especially in relation to love—be understood.

PASTORAL NOTE — **This text, in the intention of St. Paul, does not refer especially to marriage; however, it can very easily be applied to Christians who present themselves before God to consecrate this new stage of their life which they will live together. They must carry out this essential duty of love in the daily practice of conjugal love: love of the spouses, for each other, love for their children, and love for those outside their home.**

3 YOUR BODY IS THE TEMPLE OF THE HOLY SPIRIT

(1 Cor 6, 13-15. 17-20)

This text sets forth the doctrine of Christian chastity, founded upon the consecration of the human body by its incorporation into Christ, which turns it into a temple of the Holy Spirit.

Paul establishes the general principle that the body is not just for fornication, and he goes on to answer an objection based on the natural purpose of each sense, i.e., just as the belly was made for food (v 13a), so the body was made for sexual activity. He sets forth for the Corinthians who were exposed to such sophistry a very different teaching concerning the human body.

The Christian's body has a particular relationship with Christ (the Lord): Christians form the Body of Christ, which will enable them to share in the corporal resurrection. The Christian's body is directed toward the completion of itself in this adherence to Christ which makes him participate in his spiritual condition.

The exhortation to flee from fornication is based upon the same teaching: fornication is a degradation of the dignity of the Christian's body. This dignity has been acquired at a very dear price (the redemption of Christ).

PASTORAL NOTE — **This text is concerned with marriage, though not exclusively so. It lays down the general principle that any kind of immorality is bad, whether in marriage or out. However, it is not completely negative in tone. A more sophisticated congregation might well see that the body gives glory to God in the very act of marriage as well as in other ways.**

4 PRAISE OF TRUE LOVE

(1 Cor 12, 31—13, 8)

The love of God "is poured forth in our hearts by the Holy Spirit who has been given to us" (Rm 5, 5). This gives rise to the wealth of Christian love which is nothing more than the implementation of God's plan rendered present in the living activity of the believer.

The reading begins with verse 31 of chapter 12: Christian perfection does not consist in the possession of some lofty charism or other, but in the humble daily practice of love: this will never end.

Hence, the possession of all things—even those that are spiritual—means absolutely nothing.

The fundamental note of Christian love is unselfishness, which is a sign of an open and full relationship, a sign of an enriching impoverishment. Verses 4-7 constitute an explanation of this character of Christian love.

PASTORAL NOTE — **This passage has no direct reference to marriage; but it can readily be applied to it since marriage is the sacrament of Christian love. Verses 4-7—concerning the characteristics of Christian love—might well constitute a kind of directory for good conjugal understanding and to better reveal the unifying mission of the Christian home.**

5 THE GREAT MYSTERY OF MARRIAGE

(Eph 5, 2. 21-33)

The proper clarification of this reading requires three basic elements: the union of Adam and Eve to which the phrase from Gn 2, 24 refers; the union of Christ and his Church; and the union of Christian spouses. Paul sees in the story of Genesis a prefiguration of the union of Christ and his Church; a union which constitutes the great mystery revealed in the fullness of time and which is prolonged and reflected in the pair of Christian spouses.

In the Old Testament, the immense love of God for his people is frequently described under the image of marriage (Is 54, 5-7; Jer 3, 1-3; Ez 16, 8-43). This foreshadowing of the Old Testament is realized in the union of Christ and the Church (Mt 25, 1-10; Jn 3, 29; 2 Cor 11, 2; Rv 21, 2; 22, 17).

The Christian bride and groom are a living tangible reproduction of the invisible but real union of love between Christ and the Church. This reality gives rise to spontaneous conclusions: submission, love, self-surrender, and salvific mission in a renewed act of giving that will surpass all types of selfishness. The opposite would be a real betrayal of the dimension of sign and life that the marriage sacrament has, as a tangible expression of the mystery of love and giving from Christ to his Church.

PASTORAL NOTE — This is, without any doubt, the richest and most profound text of the New Testament in regard to marriage. This wealth dictates that it be used with those who possess a cultivated faith. In verse 31 we find the literal quotation of Gn 2, 24, which is also quoted in Gospels 4 and 6 (Mt 19, 3-6; Mk 10, 6-9).

6 LIVE IN LOVE AND THANKSGIVING

(Col 3, 12-17)

Family life in the Ministry of the People of God should have the following characteristics:

a) It should be presided over by love as a bond of unity among all the members.

b) The peace of Christ—that is, the friendly relations with the Father which Christ has been able to restore—must be the arbiter of the common conflicts in family life, insuring that the unity in the Body of Christ not be broken.

c) The Word of Christ should be accepted in all its charismatic manifestations.

Paul sets forth a simple family moral, but it brings the whole family to live "in the Lord," that is, as Christians.

PASTORAL NOTE — The liturgy had previously already applied this exhortation of Paul to the Christian home: it used to be the Epistle for the feast of the Holy Family.

The exhortation to mutual forgiveness will serve as a good reminder after the honeymoon is over.

7 THE UNITY AND PEACE OF THE CHRISTIAN HOME

(1 Pt 3, 1-9)

St. Peter speaks in this reading about the mutual duties of Christian spouses.

The attitude required of a Christian woman is inspired directly from the attitude of man in relation to human authority set forth earlier in the Epistle (2-13).

It stresses the value of example in proclaiming one's faith within the family circle. It is doubtless concerned especially with women converts whose husbands were still pagans and harbored the usual prejudices against the new faith. But the principle it inculcates is just as true today.

Fidelity to her husband calls for the Christian wife to practice modesty in her adornment. Her beauty should reside in inner realities rather than in an external and superfluous ornamentation of her body, following the example of the great women of the Bible.

The husband should take his inspiration from the wisdom of the gospel in order to lead a genuinely common life. He should take into consideration the more delicate condition of his wife as well as the fact that on the level of God's grace she is his equal.

The reading concludes with a call for fraternal love and all that this entails: forgiveness, unity, humility.

PASTORAL NOTE — **This reading presents a difficulty by the fact that it shows the wife in an excessively submissive position in regard to her husband. Nevertheless, it provides a good catalogue of practical and useful exhortations for family life.**

8 LOVE IN DEED AND IN TRUTH

(1 Jn 3, 18-24)

This reading calls for a love that is real and active—one not content with words alone. There is no true love of God if acts of love toward one's neighbor are lacking.

After stating this requirement, the reading goes on to speak of the "truth," that is, God himself, with an apparent lack of continuity. However, there is a certain unity involved: true love can abide only in persons who have been really sanctified by grace and move under the influence of the true God who is Love itself.

A man who lives in such a fashion also lives in complete trust. The reading concludes by alluding to the two aspects of the new commandment to love: to believe in the Son, Jesus; and to love one another. In these two basic attitudes John summarizes all our relations with God and with one another.

PASTORAL NOTE — **This reading contains no explicit reference to marriage. But it deals with the love of the partners by setting forth the general Christian teaching on love.**

9 GOD IS LOVE

(1 Jn 4, 7-12)

Communion with God makes us live his life. God is love. This love has been manifested in Jesus who went through life practicing goodness.

Fraternal love is an effect of our supernatural birth, our union with Jesus (Mk 16, 17-18) and our knowledge of the great truth: "God is love."

God gave all he had: he sent his Son to give us life. Our act of loving does not begin with us. We love because God has first loved us (Rm 5, 8-9). Our love is our response to the work of Christ who manifested his love in his complete self-surrender which went as far as his death on the cross.

To give our life for our brothers is to prolong in us the life of Christ. Jesus becomes present in us on behalf of our brothers.

PASTORAL NOTE — **Again in this reading there is no explicit reference to marriage, but simply to Christian love in general. However, since marriage is the sacrament of love, this text gives it its depth and solidity.**

10 THE WEDDING FEAST OF THE LAMB

(Rv 19, 1. 5-9)

Christian marriage is a sign of God's love for his people (Eph 5), a love reflected in the Old Testament by the idea of the Covenant (Hos 2, 16; Is 50, 1-3; 54, 6; Ez 16, 7ff; Sg) and transferred by the New Testament to the union of Christ and his Church (Eph 5, 27).

In characteristic language the Book of Revelation brings before us once again this symbol of the Christ-Church union, with an evident eschatological perspective: the wedding of the Lamb with the Church will not take place until the kingdom has definitively been constituted.

The bride wears a dress made of the finest linen and "brilliant white"—representing the virtuous deeds of the saints (the just). Contrast this with the attire of the harlot in 17, 4.

"Happy are they who have been invited to the wedding feast of the Lamb." We have all been called to it.

PASTORAL NOTE — **In order to make this text come alive for the assembly, we should emphasize the value of the sacrament of marriage being celebrated as a sign of the Christ-Church union.**

GOSPEL

1 THE BEATITUDES: THE PARADOX OF EVANGELICAL HAPPINESS

(Mt 5, 1-12)

The Beatitudes form the prologue to the programmatic discourse of Jesus which, following Matthew's arrangement we call the Sermon on the Mount.

The presence of Jesus among men is a happy sign of the coming of the kingdom of God. It forms the response to the "anawim": the poor, the afflicted and the hungry (vv 3. 5. 6; Is 58, 6-10; 61, 1-3; 49, 8-13). Thus Jesus sets forth for all ages the qualities of the disciples of the kingdom of God.

The Beatitudes directed to those persecuted for the sake of Christ correspond to a more advanced and difficult phase of his ministry.

By walking the path of the Beatitudes, the Christian goes on to meet Christ in the present and also definitive phase of the kingdom.

PASTORAL NOTE— **Although it does not refer to marriage in any special way, this text is basic for the Christian life.**

If this gospel is chosen, one should choose a reading which speaks explicitly about the sacrament.

---

2 SALT OF THE EARTH AND LIGHT OF THE WORLD

(Mt 5, 13-16)

This reading uses comparisons which illustrate the "enlightening" vocation of every Christian in the world. The words "earth" and "world" invite us all to enlarge our horizons to their highest degree.

The comparison of Christians to salt—although negative in its expression—manifests the natural need of the Christian to influence the life of others. The comparison to a city suggests the collective character of the witness that must be given.

The simile of the light shows where the essential value of the witness resides: in the expressive character of works proper to the heavenly lineage of a son of God and therefore of a brother for all men.

The splendor of God's glory is manifested in the works of his children and it invites all to meet the Father.

PASTORAL NOTE — **The exclusive use of this text over the centuries for the feast of Doctors of the Church might have led us to believe that it was directed solely to theologians and preachers. In reality, the Sermon on the Mount had as its recipients the disciples and the crowds (5, 1). The duty of witness and apostolate is thus the task of all Christians.**

3 THE HOUSE BUILT ON ROCK

(Mt 7, 21. 24-29)

The Word of God requires a decision.

The true disciple of Jesus hears his words and practices them.

Jesus is not content simply to be accepted as Lord and Teacher; he wants to lead men to do the will of the Father (v 21). This is a harsh warning for anyone who practices merely a formalistic type of Christianity. It is a call to a religion which should be not merely an external profession of, but an inner fidelity to, the Word directed to all Christians.

The final comparison stems from the customs and climate of Palestine. Genuine Christian prudence seeks—before the judgment of the Lord—a firm support; this is the result of works which spontaneously prolong a life of conscientious faith.

PASTORAL NOTE — **The application of this text to marriage is determined by the image of the house as in the previous reading. It can be chosen with the Second Reading no. 1 (Rm 8) which provides an analogous lesson although in a more difficult form.**

4 JESUS CONFIRMS THE INDISSOLUBILITY OF MARRIAGE

(Mt 19, 3-6)

The teaching of Jesus concerning the indissolubility of marriage in answer to a question of the Pharisees has come down to us in two different versions: Mk 10, 2-9; Mt 19, 3-8.

The passage chosen as a liturgical reading encloses the essence of the reply: a categorical confirmation of the indissolubility of marriage; in the very manner ordained by God when he created man.

In answer to the question put to him by the Pharisees to test him, Jesus declares what God did at the beginning and said in relation to the human couple:

—God "made them male and female" (Gn 1, 27): this emphasizes the fact that human beings were created as "male and female": the second quotation will develop the meaning of the text: the same act of creation which differentiates the sexes calls man and woman to become "one."

—Verse 5 is a consequence of the above. The attraction which draws man to woman, and woman to man is even stronger than all blood ties. The author of Genesis indicated this by Adam's words: "She is now bone of my bones, and flesh of my flesh" (2, 23); "for this reason a man leaves his father and mother and clings to his wife." Where the author of Genesis sought the explanation of a fact (man leaving those of his own blood to cling to his woman), the evangelist discovers a divine command.

After the quotation from Genesis, Jesus stresses the teaching in relation to the matter that had been put to him: divorce. Whatever destroys the unity desired by God is against all that he desires.

PASTORAL NOTE — **This text clearly and simply sets forth one of the essential requisites of any marriage: its indissoluble character. Hence, it is important to bring it to the attention of the couple and can be used with almost any assembly.**

5 THE GREAT COMMANDMENT OF LOVE

(Mt 22, 35-40)

All through the history of salvation and in diverse manners God has been revealing a Message to us: "last of all in these days he has spoken to us by his Son" (Heb 1, 2).

In this revelation of God which binds every Christian, there is a hierarchy of values. Basically, it is the sincere pledge of self-surrender to God through obedience to his greatest commandment: love for one another. This coexistence (God-neighbor) is rooted in the living practice of love for others as for ourselves (Rm 13, 8). This is the law in its fullness (Rom 13, 10; 1 Cor 13, 1-7).

A lukewarm attitude on our part toward Christ can dim the brightness of God's message and prevent us from seeing what constitutes the foundation of our life in Christ.

PASTORAL NOTE — **This is a simple text within the reach of all. It condenses the fundamentals of Christianity. It does not refer to marriage in any special way, but it can provide a splendid orientation for spouses willing to intensify their Christian life, with the sacrament as a start.**

6 WHAT GOD HAS JOINED TOGETHER LET NO MAN PUT ASUNDER

(Mk 10, 6-9)

The Pharisees set a trap for Jesus. They wish to confront him with the Mosaic law which authorizes the rupture of the marital vows (Dt 24, 1). Jesus' reply goes deep and is absolute: Moses was obliged to grant that concession because of the hardness of the Israelites' hearts.

God's will is expressed in an authentic, integral and perfect manner in Genesis (1, 27; 2, 24): marriage is a permanent union. Male and female form a new being—a new flesh. God himself effected this union, and no human authority exists strong enough to separate them. Man and woman find themselves in the same conditions. Neither is free to break his agreement (cf 5, 31-32; 19, 1-9; Lk 16, 18; 1 Cor 7, 10-11).

PASTORAL NOTE — **This is the parallel passage of no. 4 (Mt 19, 3-6). If anything, it is simpler and more to the point. It should be known to the couple and is easy for any congregation to grasp.**

7 JESUS AND MARY AT THE MARRIAGE OF CANA

(Jn 2, 1-11)

This passage is as familiar as it is obscure and discussed on account of the intermingling of its diverse strata. Mostly on the surface, there is stress on the central theme of "faith" (2, 11) as a key to the following signs (cf 2, 11 with 1, 45-51).

Deeper, and couched in symbolic language, lies the promise of the messianic gift—contained in the promise of an abundant and generous wine. (We might concentrate on this gift of an abundant and generous wine. At other times we might concentrate on this gift as a sacramental symbolism: the water is a ritual; the wine could refer to the Eucharist.) It is only a promise. The realities will be present when the hour comes (the hour of Christ's death and resurrection).

The miraculous transformation is a "sign" of his glory; the gift of the wine is a "sign" of the future. Messianic gifts in an overflowing fullness.

PASTORAL NOTE — **The Fathers of the Church made frequent use of this text to show that Jesus and Mary were not against marriage.**

Although it is very easy to do, we must avoid considering only the material aspect of a prodigy performed on the occasion of a wedding feast. The homily should not concentrate on moralizing considerations but try to show Christians the union of baptism, marriage and eucharist, the hour of Jesus: all the divine riches that Christ's intervention brings to marriage, which has been made a sign of the new Covenant, a share in the Wedding of the kingdom.

8 ABIDE IN MY LOVE

(Jn 15, 9-12)

In this framework of farewell-testament and glimpse of the future, John speaks many times of something permanent. If Jesus goes and ascends to the Father, he yet remains; not physically, of course, but in the dynamic love that lives in what it loves. Correlative love and permanence. Jesus in his followers and they in him. Or better still, projecting the line toward the infinite: Father, Jesus, and faithful.

Therefore in the disciples' sorrow over the farewell, the words of Jesus resound exhorting them to Christian joy; for precisely by his departure a more intimate and redeeming permanence is obtained—a definitive not a provisional one.

PASTORAL NOTE — **This is another text that has no direct connection with marriage. However, it consists of words of the Lord's testament which can have ample bearing at the moment when the sacrament is realized.**

9 LOVE ONE ANOTHER

(Jn 15, 12-16)

In the atmosphere of departure, the term "live on" insistently recurs in the Johannine perspective of Christ's post-Easter abiding presence in the Church. There is no sadness but rather paschal joy at this unending presence of Christ, made possible in and by the "agape," if the present and future disciples "live on in his love." And this will take place if they follow his commandment, which is none other than to embrace all the disciples in his love.

The same love embraces the Father, the Son, and all his fullness (vv 9-10). Christ has manifested it in two aspects: in giving his life (v 13), and in his Revelation (v 15). The disciples should manifest it and "love one another" and "live on in him" (the vine: cf Jn 15, 1-5) to bear fruit, to live from his life.

PASTORAL NOTE **As in the case of the previous text, this passage also does not refer to marriage in any special way; however, as a fundamental text of Christian love, basis of all marital life, it can be readily applied to the sacrament.**

10 THAT THEIR UNITY MAY BE COMPLETE

(Jn 17, 20-26)

A basic concern of John is to present the ecclesial life of his readers in the historical Jesus, together with that of his disciples. This hidden intention reaches its climax in the text in which Jesus expressly prays for the whole future Church.

Christ's relation to his Father of "living on in," being loved by" and "being one with" also extends (in an undefined manner) to his followers of every age, in a call for a radical demand for unity. This unity will be such as to become a "sign" before the world that "he was" the one God sent (v 21), and also a "sign" of the Father's love for the followers of Christ (v 23).

The unity will also concern the Glory (the way of showing men the divine majesty in the Bible) that Christ possesses with the Father, to whom he now returns, and that his followers will see by abiding with him.

PASTORAL NOTE **—This passage possesses a profound mystical richness and can underscore the unity which is to be the first aim of marriage: "The two become one flesh."**

ISBN 978-0089942-238-1
90000
9 780899 422381